PATRIOT'S PATH

Other Books by Dale Christensen

Dark Horse Candidate (2014)
– autobiography

Guide to Greatness (2014)
– inspiration to bring out the greatness in everyone

A Disciple's Journey (2014)
– spiritual perspective and religious background

Thoughts in Verse (2014)
– uplifting poetry

10 Secrets To Speaking English (2001)
– method of helping people to speak a new language

Out of Print:

The Shopping Center Acquisition Handbook (1984)
– complete process and documentation

Turning the Hearts Vol. I-IV (*1982*)
– family history from earliest ancestors to marriage

History of the Church in Peru (1991)
– selective personal and general highlights

Entrepreneur Guide: The Ultimate Business & Learning Experience (2001)
– textbook for MBA course

Teaching Improvement Program
– *USTC MBA Program & Business School* (2001)
– training for MBA professors

PATRIOT'S PATH

BY

DALE CHRISTENSEN

"I pledge allegiance to
the Constitution of the United States of America
and to the flag and to the Republic for which it stands,
one nation under God, indivisible, with liberty and justice for all."

Patriot's Path

Published by:
Dale Christensen
Books@Dale2016.com

Cover design: Matt Christensen and Rachael Gibson
Editing Assistance: Jan Jackson and Susan Allen Myers

Library of Congress, Catalog-in-Publication Data

ISBN
Hardback: 978-1-942345-04-6
Softback: 978-1-942345-05-3
eBook: 978-1-942345-06-0
Audio: 978-1-942345-07-7

Printed in the United States of America
Year of first printing: 2014

Dedication

This book is dedicated to all Patriots who love liberty and who are willing to sacrifice to protect and uphold the Constitution of the United States of America.

It is also dedicated to our children, grandchildren, and to all those who are not yet born.

This book is our way to the future, your future.

Acknowledgements

Muchas gracias to those who asked me, "Are you running to win the presidency, or are you just running to make a point?" Yes! I am running to win. But to win; I must make my point – in fact several. So before you begin reading the book, please take a moment to read *Appendix E – On the Patriot's Path.*

Appreciation to my wife, Mary-Jo, and her candid advice, encouragement, and faith in me.

Thank you also to Jan Jackson and Susan Myers for editing and making valuable recommendations, and to Ed Griggs for sharing the Chamberlain account.

Table of Contents

Preface

To be involved, we must understand, love and defend the Constitution. Being a patriot is not just a good feeling that comes around on the 4th of July. It is a fight for liberty that goes on every day of our lives. Ronald Reagan said, "Freedom is never more than one generation away from extinction. We didn't pass it to our children in the bloodstream. It must be fought for, protected, and handed on for them to do the same, or one day we will spend our sunset years telling our children and our children's children what it was once like in the United States where men were free.

You are beginning a process of learning and reviewing underlying precepts that are both eternal and constitutionally founded. The author recommends that when you finish this book, you begin to read and study the U.S. Constitution, the Federalist Papers and the original history surrounding the founding of our nation. Our future success as a nation depends on what you will do with what you learn, understand and feel. You must personally prepare, participate and develop your knowledge and skills. This will require you to identify and draft your core political values and goals.

Each of us will discover that there are Tory tendencies and habits we must give up to become a Patriot. The path is one of action on a local, state and national level. You must study, discuss, act or campaign and vote. Stay focused on the Constitution, logic and reason to avoid or overcome opposition or roadblocks.

Invite others to join you on your journey. Teach and persuade them. Encourage and support them. Help them catch the vision of where the Patriot's Path leads and how to achieve peach and prosperity by protecting liberty.

Introduction

To Whom Do We Turn?

"No Sir! I will not yield to the gentlemen from Virginia!" shouted Roger Sherman. "I will never support such a proposal that will benefit your state over mine. I will never allow for New York and Pennsylvania to dominate or rule over my smaller state of Connecticut or those of Massachusetts and Rhode Island. We are every bit as important and gave our blood and gold, as well as you! No Sir! I will not yield! NEVER!"

"Mr. Sherman, the Gentlemen from Virginia rightly desires the privilege to explain to you and to the Committee of the Whole, his rational and justification for the proposal to solve the problem that has kept us in deadlock for these past many weeks."

"With feigned diplomacy and dignity, but obvious restrained anger, Mr. Sherman responded, "Mr. President, with all due respect Sir, I have been sent here to represent and protect the interests of Connecticut and its citizens. I see no solutions to the disparity in size and population of the many states. And, there is no compromise that I am willing to make – short of postponing the issue to a further date – in having a government that dictates to me that I must work for what I have and you 'the Gentlemen of the South' purchase and own other human beings to work for what you have."

The spirit of contention prevailed and the heat and humidity of the day brought the brought the Constitutional Convention to the boiling point of explosion. Voices of opposition, threats of leaving the convention and indignations were being exchanged as the gavel was pounded. Everyone looked up to see an unfamiliar fall in the countenance of George Washington. There was a mixture of discouragement, gloom and defeat never before witnessed. His scanning glare settled on Benjamin Franklin whose cane was in rhythm and cadence with the pound of his gavel. Their eyes locked and, without words, they acknowledge to each other that they were indeed in a moment of crisis and truth, where the future of their nation lay in the balance.

"Gentlemen, please, Gentlemen! The chair recognizes Dr. Franklin from Pennsylvania." The room fell quiet as though they had been silenced by the voice of an angel. With difficulty, he struggled to his feet and then began to speak softly from where he stood.

"We have arrived, Mr. President . . . at a very momentous and interesting crisis in our deliberations . . . with a formidable obstacle in our way, which threatens to arrest our course, and, if not skillfully removed, to render all our fond hopes of a constitution abortive.

"I fear, at this time, that the members of this Convention to resolve this problem in the proper spirit. Therefore Mr. President, I propose that we adjourn for three days, to give our tempers a rest and allow time for further investigation of this subject. I also earnestly recommend that the members of this Convention do not associate with members of their own party to devise plans to cement their arguments. Instead, let them mix with members of opposite sentiments, listen patiently to their views and reasoning and try to see things from their point of view. Then, when we assemble again, I hope it will be to form a constitution, if that is possible."

All eyes turned back to President Washington for reaction, approval and guidance. They witnessed a manifesting cheerful change to light and hope. Each one in the room felt the self-same spirit and of tolerance turned their attention back to the speaker who humbly continued.

"Mr. President, I desire to suggest another matter before I sit down. I am surprised that someone else has not earlier made the suggestion. Mr. President, before we separate, I motion that we need God's help and further propose that henceforth prayers imploring the assistance of Heaven, and its blessings on our deliberations, be held in this Assembly every morning before we proceed to business. We should pray to the 'Creator of the universe, and the Governor of all nations, beseeching Him to preside in our council, enlighten our minds with a portion of heavenly wisdom, influence our hearts with a love of truth and justice, and crown our labors with complete and abundant success!' Sir, I am convinced 'that God governs in the affairs of men. And if a sparrow cannot fall to the ground without his notice, is it probable that an empire can rise without his aid?' We have been assured, Sir, in the sacred writings, that 'except the Lord build the House they labour in vain that build it.' I firmly believe this; and I also believe that without his concurring aid . . . We shall be divided by our little partial local interests; our projects will be confounded"'.

Roger Sherman quickly seconded the motion. A contentious spirit's hand was raised, but ignored. The proposal was passed and the practice followed. The delegates to the convention did as was recommended, they listened to each other and looked to God for help and the U.S. Constitution was drafted and ratified. Although he was stubborn, Roger Sherman was the only man to sign all four founding documents including the Continental Association, the Declaration of Independence, the Articles of Confederation and the U.S. Constitution. He was joined by his fellow Connecticut delegate Oliver Ellsworth in proposing what was called the "Great Compromise" designing the bicameral arrangement where the lower House of Representatives would be elected by the people of the state proportional to their population and the upper house or Senate would be elected by the state legislatures.

At the beginning of the day, he was part of the obstacle preventing progress. At the end of the day, he was part of the solution in drafting the greatest legal document ever written. Like him, we too are stubborn, but must put God first and work together to find solutions. He had no formal legal training, but was admitted to the bar, served in various public offices and private capacities. He tenaciously fought for what he thought was right, but was the first to work with others and step forward with solutions.

Greatest Weakness or Greatest Strength

There is a lot of discussion and even debate about "American Exceptionalism". Like you, I want to be on the winning team. I want to produce the most, be the best and the brightest and to win the gold. Like Roger Sherman and our other Founding Fathers, I want to fight for what I think is right, but I also want to find and be part of the right solutions.

I believe our Founding Fathers were some of the best men to have lived upon the earth. They were surely the best of their day. I also believe they were skilled and prepared for the great work they did. Yes, they were stubborn and strong willed, but they were also inspired by God because they recognized his hand in their lives and in the work they did for us. I want to be like them. And, like them, I want to be stubborn for truth and principle, protect what needs to be protected and help advance what needs to be promoted.

However, before proceeding, I must address what I think is our nation's greatest weakness and how we can once again turn this weakness into our greatest strength. Our greatest national strength is that we are the greatest nation on earth. We are the richest and most powerful nation in the world and we educate the brightest minds produce the most magnificent inventions and marvels in the world. We are the freest and most open society and everyone has the opportunity to realize their American Dream.

This is wonderful, but this greatest strength is also our greatest weakness. Why? It is because we are less grateful for these many blessings. We are forgetting God in our personal lives and in directing our nation. We are slowly losing our moral strength and too often choosing the easy path. We are expecting and even demanding what we want, when we want it and too often disregard how we get it. Bottom line, our greatest strength is becoming our biggest weakness. We boast too often and encourage too little. Pride is replacing principle. Our exceptionalism is turning us away from trying to do and be our best to comparing ourselves to others in a prideful way. Whether on the playground, in the stock market or battlefield, humility, prayer, gratitude and hope are in order. Pride can become a destructive force and will precipitate a fall as seen in the fall of many individuals and nations.

If Benjamin Franklin Were Here Today

Benjamin Franklin influenced many in stopping "taxation without representation". In 1913, the 16th Amendment to the U.S. Constitution began the insidious process of "taxation without limitation". The federal government continues to grow, to tax and to act well beyond its constitutional restraints and is gradually losing its sovereignty to global entities. The Founding Fathers would be disappointed and enraged to see the federal government as it is today.

Without a doubt, Benjamin Franklin would recognize the perilous situation our country is in today. He would describe the contention and division that exists. He would see the problems in our government as they are and recognize the need for an immediate solution. He would most assuredly propose that we turn to God for help and repeal both the 16th and 17th Amendments. He is not here today, but I am and you are. I propose – we can propose together – that we turn to God for guidance and correct this fatal error.

The very obstacle that stood in the path during the constitutional convention is the same that again stands today in the way of our progress. It is not just the need for God's help and influence, but it is also the need for a truly bicameral solution. The higher house (the Senate) needs to represent the states, not the populace. The state legislatures need to select their senators to represent the states and again provide the safety balance of power. One of the vital steps to saving the Constitution today (as it was then) is to repeal the

17th Amendment and restore to the state governments their voice and influence in the great republic of the United States of America. Until this is done, we have no hope of moving forward out of the gridlock of continuous political turmoil. There are other steps, but this the first.

I ask you to listen to my ideas. If you feel a spirit of hope and patriotism swell in your heart and light to your understanding, I ask you to second my proposal and join with me to save our constitution. I invite you to stand with me to take the other necessary steps to put us back on the patriot's path to individual responsibility, national defense, progress and prosperity.

Part I

Constitutional Guidelines for a Moral Federal Government

Chapter 1

I'm Telling You the Truth

"The further a society drifts from the truth,
the more it will hate those that speak it."
- George Orwell

Truth Is Truth

Truth is things as they are, as they were, and as they are to come. Abraham Lincoln said, "How many legs does a dog have if you call the tail a leg? Four! Calling a tail a leg doesn't make it a leg." What I share with you is what it is. You can call it what you like, but it is what it is.

While a young student attending Boston College in Massachusetts, I worked as a waiter at Boston's premier Anthony's Pier 4 Restaurant. People from all over the world worked there and dined there. One day, while working the lunch shift, I overheard a group of businessmen from New York City talking very seriously over lunch. One man leaned forward and in a very matter of fact way said, "Look, no matter how you cut it, an apple is an apple. And that's the truth!" His words impressed me, and that very afternoon I wrote the following poem:

An Apple Is an Apple

An apple is an apple, no matter what the way
You choose to eat or cut it, or the price you have to pay.
It may be green and bitter, or very sweet and red.
It may be large and shiny or withered, small, and dead.

You can carve that apple nicely or leave it there to rot.
You can bake it in the oven, or stew it in a pot.

You can share it with a neighbor and make a real friend.
It's how you use your apple that matters in the end.

Now truth is like that apple. It's very plain to see,
Whether in your hand at present or in a distant tree.

So hold to the fruit of wisdom, while old or in your youth.
Wherever you may find it, the truth is still the truth.

The Whole Truth and Nothing but the Truth

I love searching for truth and testing it to see how it works. Much of my life has been spent in sharing the truths I've found so others could have the same benefits I enjoy. It is a sacred trust to hold truths to be self-evident and to share them with others. It is also very important how I share truth, so others will consider what I offer. Each time I share a truth, I invite the listener or reader to understand it, ask questions, share concerns or rebuttal, and then find out for themselves if it passes the test of truth. However, a person's freedom to accept or reject must always be respected with courtesy and respect.

Exploring truth begins with a series of decisions, or choices. While there are different levels of knowledge and understanding, there are no conflicting truths. First, one must decide or choose to be willing to hear. Second, one must choose to open his or her mind to the possibility that what they hear and consider might be true. Third, one must choose to be willing to understand, discuss, and ponder on the facts or details of the truth they are presented and weigh it against the framework of their own belief system. Fourth, a person must choose to accept a new truth and make it part of their belief system.

There is no need to separate what you know to be true and how you live. No law or social norm should require us to separate what we believe to be and how we live unless it infringes on the rights, liberty or safety of others. What we know to be true is what makes us who we are. If we seek truth, we have no need to fear what we will find when we find it.

Sharing Truth

Abraham Lincoln gave us the key to sharing truth and freedom when he said: "When the conduct of men is designed to be influenced; kind, unassuming persuasion should ever be adopted. It is an old and a true maxim that a drop of honey catches more flies than a gallon of gall! So with men. If you would win a man to your cause, first convince him that you are his friend. Therein is a drop of honey that catches his heart, which, say what he will, is the great highroad to his reason, and which once gained, you will find but little trouble in convincing his judgment of the justice of your cause, if indeed that cause really be a just one.

"On the contrary, assume to dictate to his judgment, or to command his action, or to work him as one to be shunned and despised, and he will retreat within himself, close all the avenues to his head and his heart; and though your cause be naked truth itself, transformed to the heaviest lance, harder than steel, and sharper than steel can be made, and though you throw it with more than Herculean force and precision, you shall no more be able to pierce him than to penetrate the hard shell of a tortoise with a rye straw. Such is man, and so must he be understood by those who would lead him, even to his own best interests."

So, with that in mind, I acknowledge and respect your freedom to accept or reject what I am going to share with you. I feel strongly about these truths and principles and have a passion to share them with every American. I hope I can do it in a way that will entice you to listen and understand, consider and accept. Thank you for taking the time to read, receive, and consider these truths.

Chapter 2

Patriot or Tory

"The duty of a patriot is to protect his people from its government."
- Thomas Paine

Friendly Persuasion

A Patriot is defined as any person or public official who is loyal to the U.S. Constitution, individual rights, and the republic of the United States of America. During the American Revolution, Patriots wanted to help make their own laws, free from British subjugation. They wanted the heavy British taxes to stop. They bravely vowed to separate the American colonies from Great Britain's rule.

A Tory during the same time period opposed American independence before and during the Revolutionary War. Tories thought it best, and safest, to remain loyal to the British Crown.

It is my goal to persuade you to be a Patriot—a true Patriot—and leave behind all Tory tendencies and loyalties. To varying degrees, we all have some. It is constant work to pull the Tory weeds from our garden of freedom. It takes work to cultivate the ground and to plant and nourish the seeds of patriotism. Sometimes we go back and forth, depending on our wants and needs.

It's quite easy to get hooked on being a Tory. It takes commitment and dedication to be a Patriot. The purpose of this chapter is to help you recognize what Patriots and Tories actually are; what each thinks and feels and what decisions each makes. I hope you will see more clearly what rewards and consequences lie at the end of these two very different paths.

Recognition

Many times during American Revolution, it was difficult to distinguish who was a Patriot and who was a Tory. But, knowing the difference was a matter of life or death, victory or defeat.

Today, it is sometimes very difficult to distinguish who is a Patriot and who is a Tory. But, knowing the difference is still a matter of great importance. It will determine whether you are fighting to be free or to control others.

A Patriot does whatever it takes to defend life, liberty and the U.S. Constitution. Patriots know the difference between a democracy (rule by direct vote of the majority) and a republic (a form of government where the people elect representatives who make the laws). They don't expect a lot for themselves, but they do respect and defend the rights of others. They are ordinary people who do extraordinary things. They have a variety of talents, skills and experience. On the other hand, no matter how well educated, experienced or eloquent a Tory is, a Tory is still a Tory. A Tory is not a Patriot.

Sometimes Tories try to imitate Patriots, but want to walk a different path. They say one thing, but do something else. Once they have power and influence, they show their true colors. For various reasons, some people decide to become Tories. This is treasonous, so we must be careful and vigilant.

History of a Tory

The word "Tory" comes from the Irish word torai, meaning outlaw or robber. It was originally used for Irish outlaws or rebels before being adopted as a political label. In early American history, the term was applied in various ways to supporters of the British monarchy and those hostile to political reform.

Tories always find other Tories to support their loyalties. In mid-1800 Canada, the terms "Red Tory" and "Blue Tory" was used to describe the two wings of the elite conservative party loyal to the monarchy and adhering to British traditions in Canada.

Definition of a Tory

In the United States today, a Tory is defined as any person or public official who is loyal to personal interests, political power, party or popular philosophy above loyalty to the U.S. Constitution, individual rights, and the republic of the United States of America.

There are some naive Tories who don't realize what they are doing because they think they are acting for a good cause. However, devoted Tories are traitors to life, liberty, and the pursuit of happiness as guaranteed by the U.S. Constitution. They want power, glory and gain. Some work to destroy the liberty of the United States and of people all over the earth. These individuals and organizations and their ideology is the enemy of patriotism.

Tory Propaganda

The decline of liberty and government expansion begins with the neglect and misuse of the principles upon which that government was founded. Tories in the United States have done this by working into both the Democratic and Republican parties. They supported Keynesian economics, social reform, and eventually an acceptance of the welfare state where the government would provide most of the services for citizens.

In a nutshell, Keynesian economics is the view (attributed to British economist John Maynard Keynes) that a nation's economy can be manipulated by direct government financial intervention. It is the belief that if governments will directly stimulate economic growth they can ease the pain of unemployment, a lack of demand, and the natural cycles of recession and depression. The notion rejects the basic idea of supply and demand and a free market economy.

The theory was first presented in the mid-1930s and steadily adopted by most western governments after World War II. As I said, politicians in both major parties have sung its praises. After the seemingly permanent prosperity that America experienced during the 1950s and 1960s, Republican President Richard Nixon decided it must be because of America's adoption of many Keynesian principles. In 1971, he is even quoted as saying, "I am now a Keynesian in economics." Many declared that we are all Keynesians. January 10, 1971, Leonard Silk; The Week In Review

However, this was just prior to the oil crisis of 1973, the era of uncontrollable inflation, and other economic problems that followed. Many suddenly questioned the precepts of

Keynesian principles while others sought to perfect, reform its theories and expand its implementation to all levels. Some acknowledged that the application of Keynesian economics was easily manipulated by corrupt politicians who could distribute the money intended for economic stimulus unfairly—favoring certain companies and industries over others. My own view is that in the short run these kinds of strategies are like a sugar high or drug rush. Once addicted, the fundamentals of a healthy economy are compromised. Or to use another analogy, it's like putting your faith in vitamins, medicines, fad diets, and appetite suppressants rather than eating healthy foods, exercising, and getting the rest that the body needs.

The most dramatic application of Keynesian economics in world history may have been the multi-billion-dollar bailouts of 2007 and 2008, again favoring certain banks and other institutions while allowing others crash and burn. The end result is now the largest fiscal deficit ever experienced in American history. Some of the individuals and companies may have benefited and survived, but the federal government is the only entity that got stronger.

Today, Tories use democratic principles to promote socialism consisting of any of the various economic and political theories advocating that the government can provide for the needs of the citizens better than they can do for themselves. This also includes the collective or government ownership and administration of the means of production and distribution of goods; a system in which the means of production are owned and controlled by the state. They convince the masses that government can take care of their needs better than they can. Perhaps innocently or knowingly, they ignore the U.S. Constitutional restriction of government powers. They tend to promote expensive and cumbersome. Instead of redesigning, restructuring or reducing government in an attempt to simplify and solve, they add to, multiply, duplicate and increase government in an attempt to create more dependency.

Tories want to have power over the federal government and all state and local governments. They demand immediate gratification by imposing their solutions. They make promises of security and prosperity over defending principles of personal responsibility. Tories belittle and battle against anyone or any organization, including members of their own party, who disagrees with their views or who offer alternative solutions.

It is often tempting to use Tory tactics. We must not. There is a better way.

Tory to Patriot

A big part of the Patriot's battle for liberty is to win over the hearts and minds of Tories. This battle can be won by helping Tories understand a better way to freedom. It is done in the same way we show "enabling" family members a better way to help their loved ones overcome addictions. Big government is not the solution to our social or economic problems. Big government is the problem, because it is enabling bondage and promoting tyranny.

The battle cry of the Patriot is always to stand fast by the Constitution of the United States, to defend God-given individual rights, and to take personal responsibility for the future. Patriots will always warn others to be careful of promoting a pure democracy— rule by direct vote of the majority. The Founding Fathers did not establish a pure democracy. They established a republic—a form of government in which people elect representatives to run the country.

There are Patriots in all parties. Patriots will strive to preserve the Republic of the United States of America and protect the democratic principles upon which it is founded. The Patriot is willing to take risks and to defend the "rule of law". Rule of law means that a government leader, no matter how high up, cannot make any law or force the people to live his laws. Instead, laws are made by elected representatives of the people. Even the President has to live by the laws.

Battle Cry of a Tory

The battle cry of the Tory is always the same. They call Patriots fanatics. They mock them as being old-fashioned and selfish. Tories put party loyalty or personal relationships over principle. They want to change the world for others and promise that the government can do it better. They define classes of people and then pit one class against another. The Tory wants to redistribute wealth by taking from the prosperous and forcibly giving to the poor.

Tories want to take away the right to bear arms. This was the first thing the British and their Tory supporters tried to do to the Patriots at Concord and Lexington in 1775.

You Must Decide

It took decades for the Founding Fathers and early Patriots to convince enough Tories that there was a better way. One by one, the light of liberty began to burn in the hearts of men and women throughout the thirteen colonies. They made the decision that liberty, or freedom from British rule, without representation in British Parliament, was as precious as life itself. The idea of a Patriot's Path kept them going until they finally won the American Revolutionary War in 1783. After the war ended they worked for many years to write and ratify a constitution that set up a republic form of government.

Patriots have always paid the price to gain and maintain liberty. It always begins with a decision to be a Patriot or a Tory. You, too, must decide. What will your decision be?

Chapter 3

America's Challenges

"Our Constitution was made only for a moral and religious people
It is wholly inadequate to the government of any other. . . .
Neither the wisest constitution nor the wisest laws
will secure the liberty and happiness of a people
whose manners are universally corrupt."
- John Adams

Our Moral Compass

The surge forward in technological advancements has given the world great blessings never imagined before. However, evil forces in the world are using these same magnificent tools to promote declining morals and social problems. With every new breakthrough in information, communication, and travel we also witness evidence of the dark side. As dramatic changes in culture and social services influence more people, there is a dramatic move toward corrupted character and moral malignancy.

America finds itself in a moral dilemma and social struggle with crime, immorality and government force. America is involved in a public debate over illegal immigration, legalization of drugs and the promotion of pornography. America is struggling with protecting personal freedom and civil rights on the one hand and controlling taxes, national debt and international military involvement on the other.

Let's Be Leaders of Growth and Not Stewards of Stagnation

We are witnessing a rapid decline in respect and tolerance for marriage, families, freedom and the rule of law. Just as the climb to progress and freedom begins with a single step; so does the fall into stagnation and bondage. The only difference is that the climb is long, difficult and rewarding, but the fall is swift and devastating.

On an individual level, one's start down the wrong path may begin with just a little white lie, one immoral or jealous thought, an impulse of envy or pride or with the first sniff of cocaine. Real change begins when we stop doing bad things and start doing good things. We need to be a country of moral people, as John Adams stated.

Approach Problems Out of Love, Not Anger

We must be willing to condemn and punish evil behavior and protect the innocent. I'm not perfect in feeding the hungry, clothing the naked or visiting the fatherless, sick or imprisoned, but I try to do my best as often as I can. I try to help and serve those who are in need or are in bondage. I have weaknesses and try to repent of my sins, which are many. I cannot condemn others, but I must condemn evil and destructive ideas and actions.

In the spirit of love for my fellowman, I try to help others throw off the chains that bind them down. I make every effort to help others to realize their potential. I have had some experience counseling with those burdened with sin, addiction and guilt. I've wept with them in their sorrow, done and said what I could to lift them up. I've rejoiced in their new-found freedom. I have grown to love people regardless of their fears or problems because I consider them my brothers or sisters. We need to be here for each other. I love those I meet on the street for the same reason.

My efforts have not always met with success. But I've had enough success to know that the human spirit is beautiful and powerful and can overcome almost any obstacle. We all have sins and problems. We all live in poverty in some corner of our heart. We all struggle to get out of the bondage and slavery of our weakest thoughts or actions. We need to help each other. By helping each other, we are made stronger and better able to realize that the prize of freedom is brighter and so very precious.

Addiction Recovery

I had a dear friend whose daughter is addicted to hard drugs. There was a conflict between him and his wife as to how to show tough love and not enable her. At one point, the pattern of drug abuse was getting worse and more frequent. It was beginning to include theft, overdose episodes ending in the hospital, arrests by the police, and living with a man old enough to be her father.

Lots of time was passing with little progress. The frustration was growing. In fear and in an attempt to reach out for help, we discussed their options. I didn't know what else I could do. So, I finally had to ask him, "How do you expect your daughter to go into rehab and overcome her addiction to cocaine and heroin when you are not willing or can't overcome your addition to cigarettes and alcohol?" He was shocked by my question.

Perhaps I offended him. Perhaps you are offended. But, I wouldn't have said what I did if I didn't love him and his family. We have many addictions that rob us of our resources and self-control and keep us from reaching our potential. Someone has to say it. I hope you will consider my concerns and share your feelings with your family and friends.

Immorality Destroys Freedom and Happiness

Over the years, I have met with and become friends with many people who are struggling with sexual immorality and trying to control their appetites and passions. I love and respect them as individuals and try to understand and help. However, I don't approve of sin regardless of who participates in it. I believe immoral thought and behavior is harmful to our well-being. It is harmful to those we participate with as well as to society in general. Immorality is an influence that will tempt others, including me. I don't want that for me or for my family or others.

Dishonesty or immorality, in any form, distorts the American Dream and impedes personal and social progress. Too many lives are destroyed, too many families broken up, and too many nations decline because of immorality. God gave us commandments to help us be happy and avoid serious problems. Denying this does not relieve one of responsibility nor does it prevent the consequences resulting from immortality.

Pornography

Our natural sexuality is important and allows us to feel connection and acceptance, and to express and share these deepest feelings with another person. Many exploit this for profit by attracting us to products, lifestyles, and self-indulgence. They attempt to use our natural, neurological and physiological patterns of attraction and attachment to tie us to things rather than people. When misused or used without appropriate restraint, our healthy, normal sexuality can become an addiction.

A recent study showed that fully one-third of Internet traffic is attributable to pornography. Behind the scenes, many women and children, and some men, are victims of human trafficking and slavery. Pornographic images and videos depict relationships and behaviors that are very unhealthy, distorted, and often even dangerous. That which should be private, personal, and nurturing is being exploited for selfish purposes by users and profiteers.

Increasing numbers of experts agree that pornography harms individuals, relationships, and society in general. It affects the addicted person's ability have a normal life, keep a job, and hold together a family. This social plague is responsible for many other terrible things. By eliminating this terrible addiction, addicts will be able to overcome many other things.

How can we make good choices when our hearts are filled with lust and evil thoughts? How can men and women in responsible positions in business, politics or justice be honest and do right when they have lost their spiritual moorings and commit immoral or dishonest acts? How can we treat people with proper respect if we support this denigrating industry?

Sexuality is a private matter, but when it leaves the sanctity of our own homes and exploits the needy, enslaves the unwilling, and portrays acts of violence and harm (physical, emotional, and psychological) upon children and young people, it becomes a matter of public concern, and must be addressed through public policy in appropriate ways.

Public Trust

The question is not whether a person has made mistakes that disqualify him from deserving public trust. The issue is whether he has recognized the error of his ways, made the appropriate corrections and restitution and returned to the path of honesty and integrity. We all have sinned, but many have changed course and are diligent and disciplined in following the moral compass of truth and righteousness. Those are the people we need to find, support, and choose to be our leaders.

Chapter 4

History Digest

"I don't know how it happens . . .
but I meet with no body but myself,
that's always in the right
— Il n'y a que moi qui a toujours raison."
- Benjamin Franklin

From the Beginning

It is my hope that the following brief history will help you see the U.S. Constitution in its proper perspective. From the beginning of time we see that mankind repeatedly goes from humble beginnings to prosperity and rising civilization. This development is done by organizing governments and social networks. Then a decline always follows.

In all the recorded examples of history, we find that most men have a tendency to seek wealth, power and fame. When given a little power, people want to have more. Governments are organized to protect people and to help promote and defend freedom. However in all of these histories, we find the same repeated tendency.

Soon after defeating aggressors or tyrants, the new leaders forget their responsibility to serve and protect. They often seek more power and wealth to protect their own positions. This change in their purpose leads to additional changes in their focus. In the process, they create a new generation of rebels who rise up to overthrow them. The former rebels have become the new tyrants. This has happened all over the world.

Every Civilization

Ancient Biblical history tells of leader after leader and government after government systematically subjecting their people to bondage. This resulted in more rebellion and more war. Ancient Asian histories and Middle Eastern histories also show this same pattern repeating itself over and over again. These great civilizations all rose and then fell.

Civilization after civilization has risen from humble beginnings to power and wealth. They enjoy a period of prosperity and growth, enlightenment and liberty. Individual choices of immorality and evil inevitably lead to corruption and crime. The struggle between good and evil is no longer confined to individuals controlling their thoughts and actions. The struggle grows to involve individuals, groups and even nations. It is always a struggle between good and evil and is manifested in degrees of freedom and slavery.

For centuries known as the Dark Ages, conflict plagued the landscape of civilization. Noble and far- reaching empires broke up into feuding camps and changing territories. The names of the leaders changed, but the system of domination stayed the same. Brute force kept the minds and souls of millions in ignorance and occupied with fear and fantasy. The ruler was everything and individuals were nothing.

Religion was the government and the people lived in darkness. Wealth and power reigned over thought and reason. Ever so slowly individuals began to ask questions about the status quo and wonder if things had been better before or if they could ever be better in the future. With great opposition, the dawn of enlightenment emerged, took root and began to shine forth.

Modern History

Then a miraculous thing began to occur in the 1600s and 1700s. Men and women became enlightened with the idea of reforming civilization and religion to its prior and undefiled grandeur. The arts and sciences began to blossom and develop as never before. There was also a spiritual awakening in the hearts of many people. Individuals like William Tyndale, John Wycliffe, Martin Luther and Joan of Arc stepped forward to declare ideas that demanded changes and acted to bring them about. Many of these were martyrs who gave their lives to allow the light of truth to shine forth.

At this time, the Bible was translated from ancient into modern languages. These writings were made available to common people, not just priests, to read and understand. The printing press revolutionized civilization. There was another new era or age of reason and freedom. No longer would individuals be denied their dignity or be kept in darkness because of ignorance.

Great thinkers and philosophers began to write about the divine nature of man. They described a world where people were self-determined and equal. They replaced the divine right of rule with self-rule. The centuries-old claim of the King to divine right of rule was replaced by inalienable rights to life, liberty and the pursuit of happiness. This idea acknowledged that every individual is given divine rights directly from God. These ideas were later included in our U.S. Constitution, and in its Bill of Rights added later. We still honor and expect these rights today.

Chapter 5

Government and Religion

"We have staked the whole future of American civilization
not upon the power of the government – far from it.
We have staked the future of all of our political institutions
upon the capacity of each and all of us to govern ourselves
according to the Ten Commandments of God"
- James Madison

Why Do We Have Government?

Governments are formed for many reasons. I believe God ordains governments for the benefit of mankind. Their purposes include protection, economic development, efficiency, empowerment and social progress. Government purposes often expand to include conquering, domination, exploration and preservation.

For whatever reason governments are formed and continue, they must be controlled. Their purpose must be clear and their powers defined. If not, there will eventually occur an increase in government's size and control, accompanied by an increase in power and a decrease in accountability. Government leaders must be constantly checked, or they will grow and exert self-serving power and force. Unchecked, the role of government will quickly reverse from servant to master. This is the nature and disposition of every government.

Why Are We Free?

We are free because Patriots over the past centuries have been willing to sacrifice their resources and their lives to defend liberty. We are free because of the right choices and personal sacrifices of those who came to America long ago. We are free because our Founding Fathers were inspired by God to draft the Constitution of the United States of America. We are free because all of the thirteen colonies accepted it as the supreme law of the land.

We are free because men, women and children have chosen and continue to choose good over evil. We are good, honest, and prepared. We are free because we are willing to do whatever it takes to remain free.

In God We Trust

Why are we slowly giving up our freedom? Why are we making bad choices? Why are we willing to put ourselves into bondage through debt and addiction?

During these times, we are watching our freedom slowly slip away because we are turning away from God. More and more, we find ourselves doing evil. If we continue down this path, we will lose our freedom and way of life. This choice happens every day on an individual basis. This can also happen to us as a nation if we do not change our course. It is up to us to choose the path that will determine our future and the future of our children.

Separation of Church and State

When the Constitution was written and the republic of the United States was formed, there was still a fear that the government might someday try to impose one religion and restrict the individual's right to worship how, where or what they may. A short time later, a Bill of Rights was added. It clearly stated that government could do nothing to exert such influence. Nevertheless, there are some who want to try.

Years after the Constitution was written, the Baptist Church in Danbury, Connecticut, wrote to President- Elect Thomas Jefferson, expressing concerns about government involvement or influence in religion. Jefferson responded, "Believing with you that religion is a matter which lies solely between Man and his God, that he owes account to none other for his faith or his worship, that the legitimate powers of government reach actions only, and not opinions, I contemplate with sovereign reverence that act of the whole American people which declared that their legislature should make no law respecting an establishment of religion, or prohibiting the free exercise thereof, thus building a wall of separation between Church and State. Adhering to this expression of the supreme will of the nation in behalf of the rights of conscience, I shall see with sincere satisfaction the progress of those sentiments which tend to restore to man all his natural rights, convinced he has no natural right in opposition to his social duties."

There was no question that religion was a vital part of individual liberty and an important part of society. At that time, prayer and other forms of worship and celebration were manifested without constraint. Religious influence was understood and enjoyed by all, regardless of sect or creed.

However, over the years, poor choices were made by the branches of government, and the populace allowed it to go unchecked. There have been those who demand that prayer and religion no more have a place in the public forum. Because of not being more familiar with the Constitution and not understanding the responsibility to maintain freedom, all branches of government allowed incremental deviations to guide their thinking and actions. Instead of using a wall to protect religion from government intrusion, they use a wall to prevent prayer or any form of reference to God in government or in the public forum.

Regardless of what religion beliefs people follow, they have the right to worship and invite others to explore their religious beliefs. Private property owners can chose who they allow to enter and what may happen therein. However, public property and the public workplace are for the public and must allow freedom of speech and freedom of religious expression. To do otherwise can be detrimental to all.

Chapter 6

What Have Ye?

"Don't interfere with anything in the constitution
that must be maintained,
for it is the only safeguard of our liberties. . . ."
- Abraham Lincoln, 1856

What Do We Have, and What Does It Mean?

We live in the greatest nation on earth. Our land is beautiful. We have the greatest constitutional republic ever formed, and we enjoy freedom and prosperity. We have an abundance of food, shelter and natural resources. The American Dream is alive and well and the talents and skills of millions are apparent every day in the free market place. Today, more than ever before, any person can study, work, travel and trade as much as they want. We have abundance and more than enough.

We have the inalienable rights of life, liberty and the pursuit of happiness. We have freedom of religion, speech and press and the right to peaceably assemble and petition the government. We have the right to a militia and to keep and bear arms. We have the right to our property, privacy and possessions. We have the right to a fair, speedy and public trial by an impartial jury. We can have legal counsel and we cannot be forced to confess or condemn ourselves. We don't have to pay excessive bail or fines nor do we have to be inhumanely punished. We, the people, retain all rights not specifically given to the federal government in the Constitution.

What Do We Need?

With all the wonderful blessings, we also have some very challenging problems to solve. We have a tremendous national debt to pay off. We need to balance a reasonable and prudent budget. We need to reduce the size of the federal government by eliminating or combining some agencies and departments. Tax reform is necessary. The role of elected officials must be returned to that of serving the people and not a lucrative full-time profession. Our military must be strengthened and our sovereignty protected.

All legislation must be understandable by representatives who vote for new laws. Illegal immigration must be resolved. Voting procedures must be secured. The economy needs to be a primary focus with sound money as its base. We must bring manufacturing back to the United States. We must be environmentally responsible and energy independent. Welfare and entitlement programs must be modified and turned over to the states, not the federal government, to administer. All public officials must be held accountable for appropriate and prudent use of federal resources and funds.

Where much is given, much is expected. We should do all we can to be a good example. This is the best way to encourage freedom and democracy around the world.

Of, By, and For the People

Our government is of the people. This means that it originates from the citizens of the states and countries. Our government is by the people. This means that the people nominate and vote for the representatives who make the laws. It is organized by the people and controlled by the people, not bureaucrats. Our government is for the people. It means that it is intended to protect the people and provide an environment free of intrusion and coercion. The government is not for professional politicians or their wellbeing, or for special interests.

Inalienable Rights

Individuals are given inalienable rights from God. They do not get these rights from the government or from others. The state exists for the benefit of the people, not the people for the state. This distinction is vital to liberty and has been the point of contention for centuries. In recent decades, it is becoming more of a point of contention in the United States. Whose rights? How do the rights of one group infringe on the rights of others? These are oft-debated issues of great importance.

A Republic or a Democracy?

We are laboring to preserve our republic and our democratic principles. Our government is a republic, where citizens of all the states elect representatives to go to Washington and make laws for the country. Our government is divided into three branches, with a system of checks and balances. No one individual or branch can make the laws. Every federal law has to be approved by both houses of Congress and signed by the executive branch (the President of the United States).

Any power not specifically vested in either the state or the federal government is reserved to the people on the local level. No amount of political manipulation or long chain of precedent should change the meaning of the Constitution. No amount of conventional pomp, ceremony or celebration should replace it.

When the Constitution doesn't reflect the will of the people, their elected representatives in Congress are obligated to amend it. This process was deliberately made to be difficult. Each amendment must be approved by three-fourths of the representatives in both the House and the Senate. The validity and importance of the Constitution is compromised when politicians choose to ignore it, or interpret it broadly to suit their preferences rather than do the hard work of amending it as they should.

Rule of Law

The Constitution of the United States of America is the supreme law of the land. All laws and government activity must be guided and controlled by it. All must obey the laws passed by Congress and signed by the President of the United States. By the rule of law, no one, even public officials, are above the law.

Chapter 7

Government Threat

"The way to have good and safe government is not to trust it all to one,
but to divide it among the many,
distributing to everyone exactly the functions he is competent to.
Let the national government be entrusted with the defense of the nation,
and its foreign and federal relations;
the state governments with the civil rights, laws, police,
and administration of what concerns the state generally;
the counties with the local concerns of the counties;
and each ward direct the interest within itself.
It is by dividing and subdividing these republics from the great
national one down through all its subordinations until it ends
in the administration of every man's farm by himself,
by placing under everyone what his own eye may superintend,
that all will be done for the best."

- Thomas Jefferson

Fear of Government

When government begins to step beyond its constitutional bounds, it stops being of, by, and for the people. It stops being a servant to the people and begins being their master. Our Founding Fathers warned against this, because they feared it might happen. They tried to implement every measure to prevent it.

Then, many years later, in the 1860s, following the great calamity of the Civil War, the nation was caught up in a spirit of expansion and growth. We grew from a humble, God-fearing and family-loving nation to one of pride and ambition. We gave up the motto of "In God We Trust" and adopted the motto of "We Are the Biggest and the Best!"

The personalities of presidents and politicians have promoted this bravado approach. We outgrew the model of "defender of truth, virtue and liberty" and grew into a model suggesting "America grows everything and knows everything. Everything goes in America."

Limited Federal and State Government

As our nation grows in population and economic strength, we will encounter new challenges and new opportunities. We must continue to remind ourselves and others that the solutions are best found on the personal and local level, and not on the federal or state level. The federal government should focus on its constitutional mandate and do well what is supposed to do while being restrained from stepping beyond the bounds of its authority.

We need to remember that individuals are the lifeblood of our nation, and we need to protect them. When we have respect for individuals, we can then act in a like manner to our neighbors abroad. We can treat them the same way we want to be treated. We are responsible to our citizens and to our nation before any other nation or organization.

Checks and Balances

To help us stay focused on individual rights and personal freedom, our Founding Fathers gave us the model to check and balance government organization, government power, and political influence. Government organizations must be divided not concentrated. Government power must be limited, not expanded.

To insure this, we must be actively involved in this great cause of liberty. We must wisely select those who represent us. We must support them and help them win, so our voices can be heard. If they do not speak for us, we should promptly replace them with someone who does.

Professional Politicians

When individuals, communities and states choose political influence over patriotic principle, they are participating in the weakening of the Constitution. Some representatives and senators are re-elected over and over again because of their seniority and growing power and influence. Many come into public service with high ideals and desire to make needed changes, but the longer they are in office the more they take on the same characteristics of those they campaigned against. They slowly stop being public servants and start being professional politicians.

Many of today's professional politicians sacrifice little and demand great benefits. Too often, their loyalty is not to the people or principles, but to power or influence.

Are We Part of the Problem or Part of the Solution?

There is another test of patriotism and constitutional fidelity. We can all test ourselves individually to determine whether we are part of the problem or part of the solution. We must critically examine our attitudes and motives along with our words and actions. Do we know the Constitution? Are we congruent with its principles, or are we slightly off course? Do we use government power to do something that we should be doing with our own resources or on a volunteer basis?

If we are we trying to reduce government size, power, influence, and force, we are part of the solution. If we are promoting big government and increased government influence and force, then we are part of the problem. If we are trying to protect individual rights and promoting personal responsibility, we are part of the solution. If we are promoting government programs that take away individual rights or relieve individuals of their responsibilities, we are part of the problem.

Test Yourself

To measure your level of citizenship understanding, take the U.S. Citizenship test at the back of this book, and see how you score. To help you take these tests, use the Constitution of the United States and the Declaration of Independence included at the back of this book.

Finally, read the words to some of our patriotic songs also included in the back of this book. Listening to the music would help a lot, but as you read these words, see if you don't feel emotions welling up in your heart. The words may increase your patriotic feelings and love of country and appreciation for those who have fought and died for freedom.

Chapter 8

How Is It Possible?

"The constitution is not neutral.
It was designed to take the government off the backs of the people."
- William Douglas

How Can You Understand?

It is your right and your responsibility as a citizen to measure all political policy and every government action against the Constitution. If you do this, you can understand what is constitutional and what is not.

This requires you to read the Constitution and to understand it. Perhaps you will need to read it many times. Perhaps you will need to look up words in the dictionary to understand the meaning. That's OK, and that's what you should do. Please do it, and do it now!

Precedent

Over the years, there have been many judicial decisions to determine if laws were constitutional or not. A careful study of them will enable the ready to see where good decisions were made and where bad decisions were made. There have always been contending points of view. There have also been decisions made based on the current popularity or public outcry of an issue.

Some consider the study of law a disappointing struggle, with narrow rules and procedures or glorified accounting to regulate those in power or those without power. Regardless of how disappointing, we must take great care not to get tangled up in "narrow rules and arcane procedure." The rulings have sometimes distorted truth and complicated simplicity. It is when lawyers and judges use that one case that is just a "tiny" bit off course as precedent that we get off the path.

Then other lawyers and judges use that precedent to decide the next case, which may take the law a little further off course and so on and so on, until we find ourselves with decisions that look nothing like what the Constitution intended.

Social Justice

The Constitution intended to protect religious rights from government intervention. Ironically, some people are tempted to use this very safeguard to eliminate religious ideals from public or government forums. They then vigorously use these very religious values as their argument for forcing others to participate in activities repugnant to their conscience. They call it social justice and demand obedience.

For example, those who believe in God are asked to remove the Ten Commandments, prayer and the mention of God from public places.

> *"Let me offer you my definition of social justice: 'I keep what I earn and you keep what you earn.' Do you disagree? Then tell me how much of what I earn belongs to you and why."*
>
> \- Walter Williams

Even some religious zealots get mixed up and use social justice to force us to contribute to government charity programs. This doesn't seem to be as damaging as restricting religious worship, but it is still wrong and unjust. A well-intended, but misguided citizen said that "If you are not willing to have your taxes used to help the poor, then you are not Christian."

The Constitution does not give the government the right to take from those who have to give to those who have not. This is a result of not understanding Christianity and being led by misguided political practice.

Can or Can't – Will or Won't?

It is for all citizens to choose for themselves what kind of government they want. As for me, I choose our constitutional republic. The question is not whether we can or can't. The question is whether we will or won't.

What are our options? We can either accept what others give u,s or we can act and determine our own destiny. If enough people want to preserve our constitutional republic then we need to act, act wisely, and act now! We can begin to do this by reading and understanding the Constitution and inviting others to do the same. We can do this by campaigning, voting, and letting our voices be heard.

Chapter 9

Guide to Freedom—My Platform

"The science of government is my duty to study, more than all other sciences; the arts of legislation and administration and negotiation ought to take the place of indeed exclude, in a manner, all other arts. I must study politics and war, that my sons may have liberty to study mathematics and philosophy. My sons ought to study mathematics and philosophy, geography, natural history and naval architecture, navigation, commerce, and agriculture, in order to give their children the right to study painting, poetry, music, architecture, statuary, tapestry, and porcelain . . . The formula must provide enough government to insure order and justice but not so much government that it could abuse the people."

- Thomas Jefferson

Patriot's Formula for Freedom

The Patriot's Path to freedom offers a "Formula for Freedom." It is a prioritized game plan to save American from social programs and economic collapse. It will require some organizational restructuring, reductions in spending, and tax reform. This formula requires legislative reform, a stop to illegal immigration, and the re-development of our manufacturing base. Our monetary supply system and federal welfare program need a major overhaul.

Focus on Solutions Rather than Problems

It's easy to point to or complain about all the problems facing our nation. Bottom line, our greatest problem is immorality and lack of individual integrity. However, solving this problem is not the purpose of government. The problems the government should be focused on include: 1) eliminating the national debt; 2) balancing the budget; 3) reducing the size and scope of the federal government; 4) restoring states' rights; and 5) stopping illegal immigration.

Other important issues should be under the control of the fifty states. States, not the federal government, should focus on crime, education, and the free market economy.

A big part of the problem is the politicians and all their new legislation and regulations that make problems even bigger. Also, people are forgetting how to find their own solutions instead of depending on the government to do everything for them. Over-spending and not balancing the budget results in just "kicking the can down the road."

Experience and common sense, however, tell us that it is much better to focus on solutions than on problems. The news media sensationalize problems and tragedies, causing the whole nation to focus on them. We tend to see and get more of what we focus on. Government focuses on problems to justify its existence. Growing government requires more legislation for more government programs.

We must understand the problems, but we focus more on solutions and less on problems. If we do this, we will discover and realize even more solutions. We will need less government intervention and at the same time enjoy more personal freedom.

Resolve Rather than Revolve

Our country needs problem solvers. We have too many people merely stirring the pot. They are in constant motion, going around and around, but never resolving problems. We find ourselves at the same place where we started. It's as though we have been walking in big circles.

In an effort to solve problems, there is always more and more legislation requiring more and more money for more and more government programs. This results in more and more people expecting more and more from the government and doing less and less themselves.

The Solution

A formula to balance the budget, eliminate the national debt, and "right size" government is the only way to rebuild a robust economy. To achieve these goals, Americans need a clear vision and plan for what the solution to our problems looks like. It begins with a president who acts within constitutional limits. Outlined here is a formula for the solution to the problems:

A. The Constitution - Forward to Basics

1. Our nation's president, by law, takes a solemn oath (a sacred promise) as follows: "I do solemnly swear (or affirm) that I will faithfully execute the Office of President of the United States, and will to the best of my Ability, preserve, protect and defend the Constitution of the United States."
2. Therefore, the President's obligation, as he executes the duties of his office, is to preserve the Constitution, in other words, to do all he can ("the best of my Ability")

to not diminish it or weaken it by working against or around it, nor by stretching its meaning to suit his political agenda.

3. His duty is to protect it, or in other words, not let others work against it, around it, or do anything that would destroy it.
4. His duty is to be the greatest defender of the Constitution, against all others who's purpose it is to continually test and refine it.
5. Part of his responsibility to preserve the Constitution is to educate the citizenry about it. To encourage such familiarity with it that citizens know when their liberties, rights, and freedoms protected by it are being threatened.
6. The Constitution is the supreme law of the land; not the judiciary nor Congress, and not the President.
7. If we, as a nation, will return to the Constitution, it will outline the path we need to follow to correct past errors and point the way to go in the future.

B. Tax Repeal and Reductions

1. Repeal the 16th Amendment to return to constitutional federal funding.
2. If necessary, impose a temporary ten percent (10%) flat tax until the 16th Amendment repeal takes effect. After that, the federal government will receive its revenues from states. Each state will have its own system of raising these revenues.
3. Eliminate all subsidies and tax loopholes.
4. Eliminate savings, death and inheritance taxes.
5. Limit law suit amounts and allow interstate health care insurance sales.

C. Organizational Restructuring

1. Each branch of the federal government must act within constitutional constraints.
2. Eliminate and/or combine many government departments and agencies.
3. Immediately repeal the 17th Amendment (direct election of Senators), so state legislatures, not all the state citizens, elect Senators. This makes Senators accountable to the state legislatures. Right now, under our current system, Senators aren't effectively accountable and they embolden the president instead of protecting the states. Repeal of the amendment would once again give states more representation in the federal government.
4. States become responsible for many programs now run by the federal government.
5. Immediate hiring freeze, federal workforce reduction by attrition and reassigned as needed.
6. 10% cut in Congressional budget and eliminate perks and lifetime pensions.
7. Senators, Representatives, and all other public officials must utilize the same benefits, including Social Security and health care, as other citizens.
8. Strengthen military weapons and troops; care for veterans.
9. Reduce foreign military occupation.
10. Get United Nations out of the U.S. and the United States out of the U.N.

D. Spending Reductions

1. Reduce government spending in all departments.
2. Stop all foreign aid, including U.N. funding.
3. Use zero-based budgeting, and spend only what's in the treasury.

a. Implement a 10% cut in the Congressional budget, and eliminate perks and lifetime pensions for Senators and Representatives.
b. Start an immediate hiring freeze, resulting in a federal workforce reduction by attrition, with workforce reassigned as needed.
c. Keep only museums and national parks that pay for themselves open.
d. Users pay a bigger share of costs for public services.

E. Legislation

1. Demand legitimate legislation to be read before voted on.
2. Promote legal immigration, and end illegal immigration and require English as our national language.
3. Require Voter ID and Voter Registration along with the ability to read, write and speak English.
4. Require manual verification of vote counts in national elections.
5. Reduce litigation incentives.

F. Economy

1. Focus on bringing more manufacturing jobs back to the United States.
2. Move the nation's capital to the mid-west.
3. Establish a Composite Commodity Standard to back the U.S. dollar.
4. Audit and/or replace the Federal Reserve.
5. Review and eliminate all international treaties not in our best interest.
6. Become energy independent.

G. Welfare Entitlements

1. Use Social Security funds for Social Security payments only.

2. Phase out Social Security through attrition and a percentage reduction in benefits.
3. Phase out Medicare through attrition and a percentage reduction in benefits.
4. Allow people to plan and be responsible for their own education, medical needs, and retirement.

H. Discipline of Public Servants

1. Notify and prosecute any public official found wasting federal resources or funds.
2. Require foreign diplomats to abide by our laws or be expelled.

Cultural Shift

It is my goal, while running for President of the United States, to bring about a cultural shift. I hope to inspire other candidates to do the same. We need to bring about a vital change in the roles of our government and our government leaders.

I conclude this chapter with the words of my first campaign supporter, Lee Gibbons, who said, "In thinking about the potential campaign and my involvement in it, the thing that gets me most excited—motivated to climb this mountain—is the chance to take a bite at changing our culture, not just for the better, but truly causing it to shift forever.

"Empowering innovations bring about cultural shifts. Sustaining innovations make things better. Efficiency innovations squeeze out costs. . . . I believe American politics has been hyper-focused on sustaining and efficiency innovations that simply make things better or more efficient, but they don't enable or require cultural shift. I believe the nation is ripe for culture-shifting innovation that lifts the lid on our potential and leads us to achieve new levels of prosperity that can only be realized through the conscious exercise of our freedom, independence, and responsible use of our agency to act, and not merely be acted upon. . . ."

This lights the fires within, and I believe with all my heart that there are millions of Americans who are hungry for this cultural shift. Most of them just don't know it . . . yet!

Chapter 10

Consider the Consequences

"Government has three primary functions:
1) Provide for the military defense of the nation;
2) Enforce contracts between individuals;
and 3) Protect citizens from crimes against themselves
or their property.
When government, in pursuit of good intentions,
tries to rearrange the economy, legislate morality
or help special interests, there is inefficiency,
ack of motivation and loss of freedom.
Government should be a referee,
not an active player."
- Milton Freedman

My Invitation, My Plea, My Promise

My fellow Americans, I ask you to become intimately acquainted with the Constitution of the United States of America. I ask you to reach out to your friends and family and talk about what you learn and invite them to also read, study and understand this great and divine document. I invite everyone who will accept my invitation and challenge to pray for guidance to understand and apply the principles of this document.

I promise that if you do this, you will experience a dramatic change in your perception of truth and reality. Your mind will be filled with hope and thoughts of gratitude for the Founding Fathers and many other Patriots. You will feel a swelling feeling of love and patriotism in your heart. You will feel the same feelings that they felt, and you will have the same hope they held. You will desire to share with others what you discover.

Obvious Consequences

If we citizens of the United States do not awaken and realize the gravity of our situation, there will be disastrous consequences to pay. These consequences will include increased government control and inevitable tyranny. Personal rights will be further infringed upon and liberty will be eroded. More people will look to the government to provide for their needs. More taxes will be needed for more government programs. More and more of the people's income will go to support these government programs.

This is not our destiny. This does not have to be our future, but it will be if we do not change the course of history today. Now is your moment to make a difference on the stage of history.

Now is the time to bring about the mighty cultural shift that is needed. Now is the time to stand and be counted. The future depends upon you.

I am ready, willing and able to help you, to serve you, and to lead you. Thank you for your confidence and prayers. Together we can do it!

Part II

My Issue Statements

This part of the book is where I attempt to clarify my beliefs about issues of ideology, policy, and government. I hope that by reading them, you will get a better idea of what I hope to accomplish as your president.

1

Amendment I - Freedom of Religion and Speech

Congress shall make no law respecting an establishment of religion, or prohibiting the free exercise thereof; or abridging the freedom of speech, or of the press; or the right of the people peaceably to assemble, and to petition the government for a redress of grievances.

The Founding Fathers deliberately provided two fundamental guarantees for freedom of religion and speech. We cannot speak of one without the other. We can worship God and allow others to worship how, where, or what they may—or not worship at all. We should speak our minds and allow others to do the same without ridicule or intimidation.

I believe religious speech has priority over all other types of speech because it is fundamental to the free exercise of religion. Religious worship cannot be marginalized to the point of censorship or condemnation, or be selectively labeled as off -limits in public discussion or law making.

There is a wall of separation between church and state. This wall prevents the government from imposing a national religion on citizens. The government cannot forbid the practice of any religion. It does not prevent religion from influencing the government or being in the public arena. Laws can and should be based on moral principles.

Public debate must include religious opinion as well as public reason. One should not, and cannot, exclude the other from policy debates or law making. Religion is both a private matter and a public matter protected by the First Amendment. The framers of the Constitution never intended public reason to crowd out religion. Belief in God and religious worship is the very basis for legal and policy argument on public issues, citizen referenda, or legislative law making.

A much larger threat to free exercise of religion is federal and state actions and court decisions that attempt to subordinate exercise of religion to "civil rights." No federal anti-discrimination legislation should try to trump the First Amendment. This rightly applies to all issues.

Religious insights, values, and motives are just as important to day as they were 50 or 200 years ago. It is vital that religious belief be part of our public discourse and have equal access to the public square. This was the case with the abolition of slavery and the Civil Rights movement. These social advancements were motivated by religious principle, not just secular ethics or moral relativism. Society benefits from religion because people feel accountable to God, and thus to fair and just treatment of humanity.

The intent of the First Amendment was to protect citizens from being bullied or coerced by the government or others.

Today, freedom of speech is being diminished in private discussion and public debate. There is a chilling effect of invisible restraints and censorship of unpopular views and unwelcomed facts in the media, academia, and politics. Opposing voices are intimidated, bullied, mocked, and shouted down.

It is appropriate and vital to hear all voices in a free society. It is fundamental to the democratic process. The proper response to free speech that a person or group disagrees with is to respond with their own speech. There should never be any attempt to coerce or silence an opponent. Mob veto seeks to censor free speech.

However, the First Amendment was not intended to allow the government to permit indecency, immorality, and evil into society. It was not intended to allow individuals or groups to promote evil ideas or practices or protect evil people who pressure others into submission. Nor was it intended to allow the press itself to slander or misrepresent citizens by putting words in their mouths or bullying them.

2

Amendment II – Right to Keep and Bear Arms

A well-regulated militia, being necessary to the security of a free state, the right of the people to keep and bear arms shall not be infringed.

The inalienable right to keep and bear arms is essential to a free society. This right is also the guardian of every other right. There is an urgent need to protect the Second Amendment rights for all Americans by:

1. Repealing the "Brady Bill" and "Assault Weapons Ban";
2. Withdrawing from the U.N. anti-gun initiatives and insuring that no American tax dollars are used to fund global gun control schemes such as the "Small Arms Treaty"; and
3. Allowing pilots and specially-trained law enforcement personnel to carry firearms on board airplanes and in other public places.

3

Abortion

Human life is sacred. I oppose elective abortion for personal or social convenience. I oppose government funding of abortion. Some very exceptional circumstances may justify an abortion, but should only be considered after seeking professional medical advice. If a child is conceived out of wedlock and marriage is unlikely, I recommend adoption. There are millions of families and individuals wanting to adopt a child. The waiting list for potential parents is long.

The Declaration of Independence states one of the primary purposes of government is to protect life. The U.S. Constitution contains no right to take the life of unborn children. The U.S. Supreme Court lacks Constitutional jurisdiction. Congress has failed to declare this under Article III, Section 2, Clause 2 which states, "In all the other Cases before mentioned, the Supreme Court shall have appellate Jurisdiction, both as to Law and Fact, with such Exceptions, and under such Regulations as the Congress shall make."

The Roe v. Wade ruling is not supported by the text or constitutional principles and should be overturned. Arguments for abortion are flawed. At its core, elective abortion is fundamentally evil and is an assault on the sanctity of innocent human life. The original Hippocratic Oath forbade abortion. Destroying a human fetus is destroying a human being. Abortion causes spiritual, emotional and psychological damage in the lives of all participants. It is unconstitutional to use federal money for abortion.

4

Agriculture

Agriculture is fundamental to the American way of life. It is large enough and strong enough, with ample information for producers to regulate itself as an industry. Farmers don't want subsidies. They want fair market value for their products at market. Government should never pay farmers not to produce. The American agricultural industry should not be a political or partisan issue. It should be an individual issue, and it should not be for sale to benefit special interests over individual or national interests. Social welfare programs such as food stamps, etc. should not be part of the political agriculture landscape.

5

Balanced Budget

A balanced budget and reduced federal spending is the only way to stay free from bondage and to maintain a robust economy. However, a "Balanced Budget Amendment" to the constitution is not wise. Such an amendment would only justify increased taxation and increased spending.

To reduce federal spending and achieve and maintain a balanced budget and we must:

1. Dramatically reduce government spending in all departments and eliminate or combine some government departments.
2. Implement an immediate hiring freeze and make a reduction and reallocation in the federal workforce and

in Congressional paychecks and perks and eliminate lifetime pensions for government workers.

3. Eliminate corporate, farm, and other industry subsidies.
4. Stop foreign aid.
5. End foreign military intervention and reduce foreign occupation.
6. Use zero-based budgeting to plan for necessary expenditures one year in advance, and collect revenues based on these needs.
7. Spend only revenues already in the treasury.
8. Honor commitments to veterans.
9. Repeal the 16th Amendment to take effect in five years (December 31, 2021), with a temporary amendment for a flat tax of ten percent on all incomes until that date. After that date, the federal government will be funded by the states. Each state will determine its own way of raising funds.
10. Repeal the 17th Amendment, so state legislatures, not the public, elect Senators. This makes Senators accountable to the state legislatures. Under our current system, Senators aren't accountable to anyone. Repeal of the amendment would return the balance of power and once again give states more representation in the U.S. Senate.
11. Phase out Medicaid through attrition and a percent reduction in benefits.
12. Phase out all federal entitlement programs after three (3) years, and make states and communities responsible for their own assistance programs.
13. Abolish savings, investment, and death taxes.
14. Limit liability suit awards.
15. Allow health insurance to be sold to individuals and across state lines
16. Audit, reform, or replace the Federal Reserve with

appropriate currency legislation to strengthen the dollar and stabilize inflation.

17. Establish a Composite Commodity Standard to value the dollar (including precious metals, grains, natural resources, stock/bond market, GNP, bit coins, foreign currencies, etc.).

6

Commodity Composite Standard

The U.S. dollar needs to be backed by a "Composite Commodity Standard" that is regularly re-evaluated. This standard should include precious metals, grains, livestock, natural resources, government trade, stocks/bonds, real estate, bit coins, foreign currencies, etc. Perhaps the precious metals and natural resources should be related to or adjusted according to the annual production of renewable grains. For example, 20, 50 or 100 items could be selected according to their stability as ingredients in at least 10 different categories of this composite commodity standard.

7

Congressional Reform

Serving in Congress or as President is an honor and a service, not a career. The Founding Fathers envisioned citizen legislators and presidents. Elected officials should serve their term(s), then go home and go back to work. All the following suggestions should be implemented according to the strict interpretation of the Constitution:

1. Government executives (Congressmen, Senators, Presidents, Vice Presidents and Cabinet members) should collect a salary while in office, but receive no pay when out of office. Repeal related amendments and require each individual to be responsible for their own retirement.
2. All government executives (past, present, and future) should participate in Social Security and move all of their current and future congressional retirement funds immediately to the Social Security system, as long as other workers are required to contribute to the Social Security system.
3. Government executives should purchase and develop their own personal retirement plans, just as other Americans do.
4. Government executives should no longer vote themselves a pay raise. Congressional pay should rise annually by the lower of either a Consumer Price Index (CPI) or 3%.
5. Government executives should participate in the same health care system as other Americans.
6. Government executives should abide by all laws imposed on the American people.
7. All contracts with past and present government executives should be void effective immediately. The American people did not make this contract. The executives made these contracts with and for themselves.

8

Debt Ceiling

There should be no continuing debt ceiling because there should be no continuing debt. If we are the greatest nation on earth, why are we in debt? Except in time of declared war, if the deficit is more than three percent (3%) of the Gross National Product (GDP), then all sitting members of Congress should become ineligible for re-election.

9

Economy

In order to end the economic crisis of inflation, budget deficits, bailouts, and declining dollar value, we need to:

1. Balance the budget;
2. Lower or eliminate the debt ceiling;
3. Audit or reform the Federal Reserve;
4. Legalize sound money by returning to a commodity standard;
5. Become energy independent (see Energy below)
6. Replace income tax with a 10 percent flat tax for a number of years;
7. Support small business development and growth.

The key to American prosperity is to implement lower taxes, limited government, and sound money based on a commodity standard. We will thrive again when we all work together to reform taxes, spending, monetary policy and domestic relations.

Tax reform should include incentives to invest and grow companies and create jobs. Individuals and companies should be motivated to save money and purchase homes. Death and inheritance taxes and other such double taxation should be eliminated.

Spending reform should include freezing non-defense and non-entitlement spending and reducing overseas military commitments while building up weapons, bases, and troops on our own soil.

Monetary policy reform should include televised open market committee meetings of the Federal Reserve. All Board of Governors of the Federal Reserve should continue to make weekly information reports. Bring jobs back to the United States by supporting innovation, production and small business development. All costly and unnecessary regulations should be identified, evaluated and removed. States and municipalities should monitor, regulate and help their own citizens and businesses. Individuals and businesses need access to credit and capital through community banks, credit unions and other financial institutions to foster economic growth, serve their communities, boost small businesses and increase individual savings.

10

Education

Parents should have the greatest influence over the education of their children and should have the freedom to choose the best educational options. No amount of big government spending can or will solve our nation's education problems. One size fits all does not work. It is parents, together with the educators they choose, who will solve those problems.

Home Schooling is a viable and effective alternative to traditional or public education. It can be superior in some ways due to its unique advantages. Families who homeschool their children should not be penalized. Home schooling diplomas should be treated on par with traditional diplomas.

11

Election Reform and Ballot Access

When the Founding Fathers began this great experiment of governing a new country, there were many political parties who worked out their differences by following the Constitution. Slowly, parties began to lose strength or to align themselves with one another because of state laws favoring those in power. Our democracy is no longer one of many voices, but of only two voices—Democrats and Republicans. Our federal ballot access laws are intentionally written to support a two-party system.

In comparison to all other democracies in the world, the United States has the worst ballot access for political candidates. It is difficult for potential candidates to get their names on ballots. Each state makes its own laws describing how a person can get his or her name on a ballot. Because there is no single standard for the whole nation, the general public and media are generally ignorant about ballot access laws.

A "sore loser" is a candidate who is defeated in a party primary, but desires or is encouraged to continue to run as an independent. Sore loser laws are designed to protect the two major political parties to rule without dissent. Only Connecticut, Iowa, New York and Vermont allow sore losers to continue to run as Independents. This is not fair, nor is it democratic. Both the Republican and Democratic parties promote democracy. Yet both continue to use these laws to their benefit.

Today, approximately one-third of all state House elections are unopposed and end up being one-candidate races. Ballot access laws need to be reconsidered and election reform discussed. If this does not happen, the democracy we know today will only sway back and forth between two opposing ideologies who will continue to impose their will on the other when they are in power.

Another aspect of election reform that should be addressed is term limits for members of the House of Representatives and U.S. Senate. It was never intended for these representatives to be professional politicians. Term limits will help the people take power back from the federal government and give it to the people on the state and local level.

12

Energy

Everyone will benefit if we promote free-market solutions to our nation's energy needs instead of allowing government regulations, subsidies and taxation to control domestic production. Heavy tariffs should be imposed on foreign oil imports.

The answer to our energy independence is to purchase and/or produce domestic alternative fuel/energy technologies. Restrictions on domestic and off-shore drilling and use of coal and nuclear power should be focused on safety and environmental protection, not on volume of production.

There is nothing wrong with being pro-environment and pro-development. We need energy independence and growth!

Energy independence is the future. Energy touches every aspect of our lives. It lubricates the gears of our economy. Our prosperity has been driven by steady, abundant, affordable energy supplies. There are many more yet to be developed.

13

Entitlements

Government entitlements foster negative and unproductive ideas and practices. One such idea is, "I cannot change. I am a victim of my circumstances." This is a destructive philosophy that encourages isolation, fear and resentment. It causes one to dwell on being a victim. This belief tortures and destroys people as prisoners of their own thoughts. It produces supporting attitudes and habits that are passed on to following generations. Government programs try to change those in poverty by putting them in a different environment. Victims remain victims in their new environment.

Freedom from this kind of entrapment comes when people accept responsibility for their thoughts, actions and future. They become enlightened when they realize that they cannot control everything that happens to them, but they can always control how they react to what happens. Hope and faith is born in this realization. We can stand and fight and overcome our weakness when we take ownership of our own lives. This is personal liberty. No one can give it to us and no one can take it away from us, but it is something that we must at times fight for in our own minds and hearts.

14

Environment

There is no question that pollution is a serious problem. Whether or not it is causing global warming is not the right question. The right question is who can and should control the environment and pollution. God is in control of the environment. We are in control of pollution. At this time, with our current pollutant levels, individuals and their respective states should control their pollution and manage their natural resources. Property owners and their respective states should be able to hold polluters accountable in their local courts. Pollution control should not be under control of the federal government.

15

Espionage

The federal government should not gather intelligence or spy on citizens or use public funds to influence citizens. It should not participate in cyberwarfare. It should not monitor, lure, degrade, discredit or sometimes destroy targets without a Declaration of War. Federal agencies should act under congressional oversight, with limited budgets and missions. They should not act illegally under the cloak of national interest or infringe on free speech and privacy, or use deception.

16

Federal Reserve

The Federal Reserve needs open and comprehensive audits and restrictions on making deals with foreign and domestic banks and interfering with the free market system by manipulating interest rates and directing the U.S. Treasury as to how much money to print and coin. In the Constitution, Section 8, Congress was given these powers. Congress needs to take back its rights, shoulder its responsibilities, and manage the Federal Reserve or end it.

17

Foreign Aid

There is no constitutional authority for giving foreign aid. Foreign aid does not buy friendship or goodwill. Foreign aid promotes central planning, socialism, dependency and poverty. It results in tremendous inefficiencies, waste, friction and hatred.

18

Health Care

Americans deserve a government that "does not harm" their health care. Patients should receive the best care available. The doctor-patient relationship is vital and must be protected. Cost and liability are looming issues to be addressed. The question is how all this is to be accomplished.

First, re-draft the Affordable Care Act (called ObamaCare) into a legitimate and understandable law. Keep the best and discard the rest. No one wins where there is excessive government control and forced mandates. Such intrusions force doctors to move from a patient-care model to business-care model. Insurance becomes more expensive to purchase and more difficult to maintain. Politicians trade influence for favors. Patients are left less protected and more frustrated. Industry oversight, reasonable limits on litigated damages, and doctor-patient shared malpractice insurance are part of the formula.

The Food and Drug Administration (FDA) and the Federal Trade Commission (FTC) should not be interfering with Americans' knowledge of and access to alternative treatments and to dietary supplements. The collusion of these organizations and large pharmaceutical companies keeps many valuable and needed cures from the market.

The answer to our nation's health crisis lies in freedom – not force. Insurance should be available for purchase across state lines. All Americans should be eligible for Health Savings Accounts (HSAs) and government-imposed barriers for the same should be removed. Everyone should pay a modest amount into an insurance fund used for catastrophic emergencies and terminal illness. In special cases, family, friends, communities or charitable organizations should help, but not the federal government. Finally, monies paid for Medicare and Medicaid should be safeguarded and not be used for any other purpose.

Forgive me for some "healthy" humor in sharing the longest sentence in competition with this piece of legislation. The following is self-explanatory: "We are going to be gifted with a health care plan we are forced to purchase and fined if we don't which purportedly covers at least 10 million more people without adding a single new doctor but provides for 16,000 new IRS agents written by a committee whose chairman says he doesn't understand it passed by a congress that didn't read it but exempted themselves from it and signed by a president who smokes with funding administered by a treasury chief who didn't pay his taxes for which we will for which we will be taxed for 4 years before any benefits take affect by a government which has already bankrupted Social Security and Medicare all to be overseen by a Surgeon General who is obese and financed by a country that's broke." So what the BLANK could possibly go wrong?" Dr. Barbara Beller

19

Immigration

I am in favor of legal immigration. This is a great and promised land and blessed above all others. We should invite those who love liberty, religious freedom and want to work and prosper to come and join with us as patriotic citizens. But let them come for these reasons and with a determination to become an American. Let them come to pledge allegiance to the Constitution of the United States of America, to the flag and to the Republic for which it stands. Let them come to learn English and to be loyal to no other country.

The United States has created several immigration problems that need to be addressed:

1. Keeping families together for immigrant workers who were encouraged to come and work, but not given permanent status;

2. Lack of documentation process or immigration law enforcement for those who came or stayed illegally;
3. Allowing children to be born to illegal immigrants in the United States;
4. Federal, state and local permissive approach to addressing illegal immigration issues.

We should promote legal immigration and end illegal immigration in order to:

1. Protect our citizens, economy and culture;
2. Prevent our country from absorbing illegal aliens;
3. Stop the financial drain and negative impact on our economy;
4. Begin receiving economic vitality and revenues from happy and productive workers.

We can achieve this by doing the following:

1. Respect states' rights and American citizens' civil liberties.
2. Promote legal immigration and punish illegal immigration.
3. Secure all boarders and points of entry.
4. Deport all who have criminal records.
5. Establish English as the national language to insure cultural integration and loyalty to the U.S.
6. Document immigrants for travel, work, and voting status.
7. End all social benefits for illegal aliens.
8. Grant legal work status to persons arriving and living in the U.S. prior to a specific date.
9. Allow those granted legal work status three (3) years from a specific date (see #8) to apply for citizenship, behind those already legally in line.

10. If those granted have not qualified for citizenship by a specific date (see #8), they will be deemed illegal aliens.
11. Those arriving without proper visas on or after a specific date (see #8) will be considered illegal aliens.

We must monitor and limit legal immigration until we are ready to assimilate additional citizens into our economy, society and culture. Allowing illegal immigration will not solve world poverty nor will it enrich our nation. We can best help other countries by being a good example and teaching self-reliance and serving them of our own free will and not by government foreign aid.

Let us follow Theodore Roosevelt's challenge of 1907, "In the first place, we should insist that if the immigrant who comes here in good faith becomes an American and assimilates himself to us, he shall be treated on an exact equality with everyone else, for it is an outrage to discriminate against any such man because of creed, or birthplace, or origin. But this is predicated upon the person's becoming in every facet an American and nothing but an American . . . There can be no divided allegiance here. Any man who says he is an American, but something else also, isn't an American at all. We have room for but one flag, the American flag . . . We have room for but one language here, and that is the English language . . . and we have room for but one sole loyalty and that is a loyalty to the American people."

20

Jury Nullification

Jury nullification is the right of a jury to acquit a defendant they believe to be guilty if they disagree with the law or application of the law that the defendant has been charged with breaking. A jury can similarly convict a defendant on the ground of disagreement with an existing law, even if no law is broken. In jurisdictions with double jeopardy rules, a conviction can be overturned on appeal, but an acquittal cannot be overturned. A jury verdict contrary to the letter of the law pertains only to the particular case before it. A pattern of jury nullification may indicate public opposition to an unwanted legislative enactment.

Jury nullification is a "de facto" power of juries. Judges rarely inform juries of their nullification power. The power of jury nullification derives from an inherent quality of most modern common law systems of a general unwillingness to inquire into jurors' motivations during or after deliberations. A jury's ability to nullify the law is further supported by two common law precedents: 1) the prohibition on punishing jury members for their verdict, and 2) the prohibition on retrying defendants after an acquittal (double jeopardy).

Jury nullification is the source of much debate. Some maintain that it is an important safeguard of last resort against wrongful imprisonment and government tyranny. Others view it as a violation of the right to a jury trial that undermines the law. Some view it as a violation of the oath sworn to by jurors. In the United States, some view the requirement that jurors take an oath to be unlawful in itself, while still others view the oath's reference to "deliverance" to require nullification of unjust law.

By taking the oath, the jurors commit that they "will well and truly try and a true deliverance make between the United States and the defendant at the bar, and a true verdict render according to the evidence, so help [me] God." United States v. Green, 556 F.2d 71 (D.C. Cir. 1977).

Some fear that nullification could be used to permit violence against socially unpopular factions. They point to the danger that a jury may choose to convict a defendant who has not broken the letter of the law. However, judges retain the rights both to decide sentences and to disregard a jury's guilty verdicts, acting as a check against malicious juries. Jury nullification may also occur in civil suits, in which the verdict is generally a finding of liability or lack of liability (rather than a finding of guilty or not guilty).

Despite debate, there is little doubt as to the ability of a jury to nullify the law. Today, there are several issues raised by jury nullification, such as whether:

1. Juries can or should be instructed or informed of their power to nullify;
2. A judge may remove jurors "for cause" when they refuse to apply the law as instructed;
3. A judge may punish a juror for exercising the power of jury nullification;
4. All legal arguments, except perhaps on motions at the start of the trial to exclude evidence, should be made in the presence of the jury.

Juries were originally composed primarily of "laymen" from the local community. They provided a somewhat efficient means of dispute resolution with the benefit of supplying legitimacy and proving guilt. Over time, juries have tended to favor the "not guilty" verdict over "not proven" and with this the interpretation has changed. Now the "not guilty" verdict has become the normal verdict when a jury is convinced of innocence and the "not proven" verdict is only used when the jury is not certain of innocence or guilt.

In the 21st Century, many discussions of jury nullification center on drug laws that some consider unjust either in principle or because they are seen to discriminate against certain groups. Approximately 3-4 percent of all jury trials involve nullification. A recent rise in hung juries is seen by some as being indirect evidence that juries have begun to consider the validity or fairness of the laws themselves.

The Supreme Court has held that trial judges have no responsibility to inform the jury of the right to nullify laws. This decision, often cited, has led to a common practice by United States judges to penalize anyone who attempts to present a nullification argument to jurors and to declare a mistrial if such argument has been presented to them. In some states, jurors are likely to be struck from the panel during voi dire (process of choosing jurors) if they will not agree to accept as correct the rulings and instructions of the law as provided by the judge.

Generally, juries are instructed to serve only as "finders of facts", whose role it is to determine the veracity of the evidence presented, and the weight accorded to the evidence, to apply that evidence to the law and reach a verdict, but not to decide what the law is. In recent rulings, the courts have continued to prohibit informing juries about jury nullification or removing them from the jury if they understand their power to nullify. This trend is not to the benefit of liberty and justice for all.

21

Leadership

Leadership is all about giving vision, inspiring and showing the way. Leaders do not solve problems for others, but help others solve their own problems. They enlighten others, give them opportunities according to their capacity and then allow them to grow stronger. They follow up and encourage personal development and dependence on a power higher than themselves.

Traditionally, and especially today, education, experience, intelligence and success are typical qualities that distinguish strong leaders. However, there are other qualities that are also valuable and important. These qualities include example, patience, service and sensitivity. Some of the greatest leaders have emerged when poor, uneducated and inexperienced individuals have stepped up to the challenges that others were not willing to accept or correctly address.

Good leaders do not seek power, but want to control it. They seek freedom. They are selfless instead of selfish. They do not seek status. They seek to serve. They are not concerned about their own needs. They are concerned about the needs of others. They do not seek to manipulate or control others. They seek to develop others. They do not act with harshness or injustice. They act with a balance of compassion and justice.

National leadership is all about looking to the Constitution for guidance. It is upholding and defending it and being willing to be limited by it. Leaders who are true to the Constitution will be true to individual rights and to life and liberty.

22

Legitimate Legislation

No bills should be signed into law that have not been read and understood by all who vote on the same and by the "reasonable person." Bills should rarely be longer than the U.S. Constitution itself. Each legislator should read and understand the bill before debating it and voting on it. This can easily be determined by their declaration in good faith, along with a brief quiz and affirmation that each legislator can perform prior to presenting it before the floor for debate and vote. The bills and the results of such examination should be part of the public Congressional Record. Each public servant should be held accountable for their public stewardship.

23

Made in America

The United States has lost millions of manufacturing jobs to foreign countries due to this country's unfriendly business climate and excessive government regulations. American citizens can now make a huge difference in our economy by buying "Made in America" products. Quality and worker productivity is still the hallmark of the American way of life. And, with stagnant wages and an abundance of cheap oil and natural gas, the United States could be on the threshold of experiencing a rebound and rebirth in manufacturing and emerging market growth. The challenge will be to improve the business climate by dramatically reducing government intervention.

We can win back manufacturing jobs to America with innovation, engineering design, retooling and developing free-market supply chains. Dynamic technology and sourcing techniques that allow an alliance between supply and demand will also allow foreign companies to be closer to consumers. Providing access, real-time communication and collaboration will allow U.S. manufacturers to compete globally by meeting production and time-to-market expectations of cost, quality and delivery.

Rising wages, fuel and transportation costs and intellectual property risks are causing domestic and foreign companies to consider American production as a viable alternative. The U.S. is still a huge consumer market, and producers want to be able to deliver their products quickly and cheaply.

24

Marriage and Fidelity

Marriage between a man and a woman is ordained of God. Any sexual activity outside of marriage is wrong and should be condemned. Same-sex marriage should not be recognized, but other rights of same-sex individuals for housing, employment, etc., should be supported. It is not a sin to have feelings toward another who is not your spouse, only in yielding to such temptation.

All parties have constitutionally protected rights to express and advocate their convictions. All parties should show respect and civility to one another, even if they disagree.

25

Military Academies

All foreign exchange programs with our military personnel should be on a graduate level at public and private universities or in a graduate military program, but not in our military academies. First preference to academy cadet acceptance should be given to enlisted personnel or veterans, and then to high school graduates. All clothing, products and paraphernalia used on campus and sold in the gift shop should be made in America.

26

National Defense

National defense is the primary purpose and responsibility of the federal government. It should be strengthened by focusing on protecting national interests at home, and not on foreign involvement. A strong military is strengthened by an armed citizenry and by protecting their Second Amendment (right to keep and bear arms) and Fourth Amendment (freedom from unreasonable search and seizure) rights.

The Transportation Security Administration (TSA) should be eliminated. Secure borders, economic stability, citizen integrity, and national unity are all essential to a strong national defense. Wars will be prevented or won by requiring the President to define victory along with a clear mission and strategy and requiring Congress to make its declaration

27

Presidential Duties

During the 1900s, U.S. Presidents gradually began to act beyond their constitutional authority on the one hand, and neglected to do their their constitutional duty on the other. The President should be to be disciplined enough to act, but only within the constitutional powers of the office.

According to the U.S. Constitution, the President of the United States has ten basic responsibilities:

1. Serve as Commander in Chief of the armed forces
2. Grant reprieves and pardons except for cases of impeachment
3. Make treaties, "provided that two-thirds of the Senators present concur"
4. Appoint ambassadors, ministers, Supreme Court justices and other officers
5. Fill vacancies during Senate recess
6. Give the State of the Union address and recommendations from time to time
7. Convene one or both houses of Congress and adjourn them
8. Receive ambassadors and other public ministers
9. Faithfully execute the laws
10. Commission all federal officials and officers of the United States

28

Religion

"Congress shall make no law respecting an establishment of religion, or prohibiting the free exercise thereof." I worship God, and I am a disciple of His Son, Jesus Christ. I strive to follow Him in all I do. I respect and defend the right for all individuals to worship or not to worship according to the dictates of their own conscience. I encourage people of all faiths, sects, parties or denominations to believe as they wish, to worship, and o live according to their moral codes. I invite all to be respectful and tolerant of the beliefs of others.

While it may be popular at times to keep faith and religion for private and personal reflection only, I follow the Founding Fathers' zeal to proclaim faith and promote religion and true principles. When any individual, group or religion tries to force their religion, or their opposition of religion, on others through legislation or coercion, it is my duty to protect those being forced and defeat those who force.

29

Right to Work

Freedom of association is a right protected under Amendment I. Individuals should be able to work where and how they choose and to join unions to influence work safety and honesty. However, no individual should be forced to join or pay union dues in order to work. Union workers should be able to participate in fair and open elections of their leaders.

Federal minimum wage and child labor laws impede personal incentive and economic progress, and should be eliminated and left to states and municipalities to monitor.

30

Social Security and Medicare

Use Social Security and Medicare funds for Social Security and Medicare purposes only. Phase out Social Security and Medicare through attrition and a percentage reduction in benefits within a designated period of time. Allow people to plan and be responsible for their own education, medical needs and retirement.

Social Security contributions would remain the same for 10 years. However, Social Security benefits will be gradually phased out by reducing benefit payments on a percentage scale over the same 10 years.

- 80+ years + sacrifice 10%
- 70-79 years + sacrifice 20%
- 60-69 years + sacrifice 40%
- 50-59 years + sacrifice 50%
- 40-49 years + sacrifice 60% w/conversion option (lump sum payment)
- 30-39 years + sacrifice 80% w/conversion option (lump sum payment)
- 20-29 years + sacrifice 90% w/conversion option (lump sum payment)
- Under 20 years sacrifice 100% w/no new Social Security or Medicare participants.

After 10 years, eliminate Social Security altogether. In the meantime, allow everyone to choose Social Security or opt out and invest the amount in their own retirement programs.

31

State's Rights

States should take the responsibility for many of the departments and programs now run by the Federal Government, including education, health, and welfare.

Repeal Amendment 17. Senators should represent, and be elected by, the members of the legislatures of their states in order to preserve a balance of power between the federal government and the states. Currently, Senators are elected by direct vote of the citizens of each state.

32

Tax Reform

Repeal the 16th Amendment to the U.S. Constitution (Graduated Income Tax). If a transition period is necessary, then replace it with an amendment that reads, "The Congress shall have power to lay and collect a ten percent (10%) tax on incomes until December 31, 2017, from whatever source derived, without apportionment among the several States, and without regard to any census or enumeration. On January 1, 2018, the 16th Amendment is repealed." This will eliminate taxation without limitation and again allow states to check federal runaway spending.

33

United Nations

There is no justification or advantage for the United States to be involved in the United Nations. There is very little to gain and much to lose. The United States gives foreign aid to have other governments finance their U.N. representatives to come and live in the U.S. and promote the U.N. agenda. The U.N. entangles our foreign diplomats and military forces in projects and offensives that we have no business being involved in.

The United Nations' charter is a charter fostering turmoil around the world and of undermining the sovereignty of the United States. Its intent is to have growing global influence and control and dominion over all other nations. Although it appears to have many good intentions, it is very ineffective in accomplishing these goals and uses them to front other unconstitutional initiatives. It is a forum for many individuals and organizations to weaken the strength of our republic and undermine our national security.

The following urgent measures need to be taken: a) stop U.S. funding of the U.N.; b) eliminate diplomatic privilege and immunity to U.N. members, staff and their dependents; c) move the U.N. headquarters out of the U.S.A.; and d) withdraw as a member of the U.N.

Part III

Speeches

Speech #1

The Constitution, Divinely Inspired

A Simple Society

In a simple society with just a family, or a small group, there is really no need for a formal government. Historically, all believed in a Supreme Being, referred to as God, though God was called by various names, depending on the time and place. The decisions were made and actions were judged based on what the people believed God wished them to do, or commanded them to do.

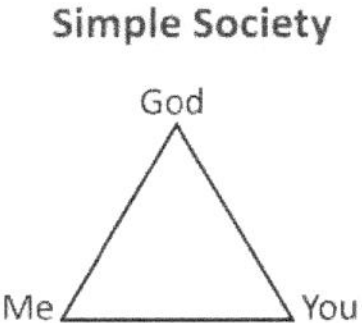

Need for Government

As the population increases and spreads out over a broader geographic area, there is a natural tendency for individuals to group together into tribes or communities. The perception of God changes, and the understanding of what is expected or commanded also changes. This commonly results in disagreement and conflict. When this happens, there is a need for conflict resolution and protection.

Divine guidelines are supplemented by additional laws designed by people. These laws become more rigid and are subject to change, depending on the mind and will of the people. The various forms of government have evolved. In this model, government is a tool or servant of the people to help them promote peace and protect individual freedom of worship, speaking out, and defending themselves, etc.

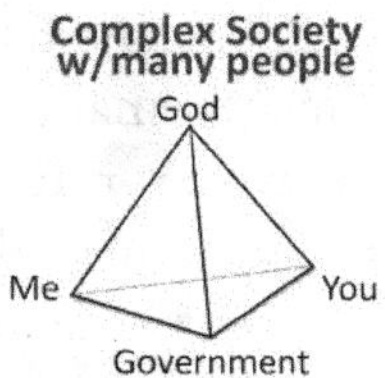

Secular Societies

When a large number of any society places more emphasis on people's laws over God's laws, there are dynamic cultural changes, resulting in dramatic shifts in the role of government. When government replaces God in society and in the minds of the people, God becomes someone from whom we simply receive comfort and rely on in affliction. Religions and churches are formed so like-minded people can worship according to their will. Secular governments begin to view religions and churches as a crutch for the weak and dependent.

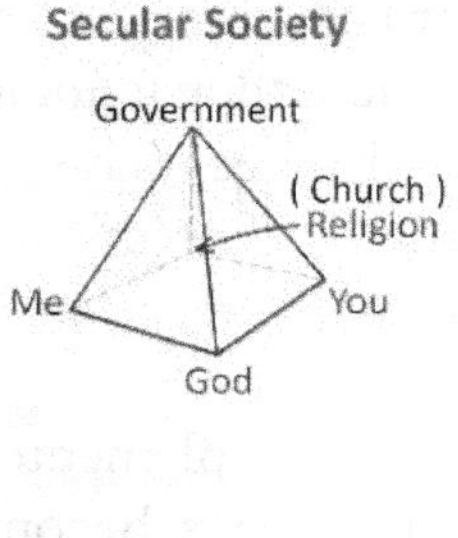

Secular Society

Government
(Church)
Religion
Me
You
God

Need for Revolution

When government becomes the master and the people become its servants, God sanctions and supports the right of the people to revolt and put both God and government in their rightful place. It is not only a divine right, but it is a noble and compelling responsibility for people to fight for and protect freedom. Such was the case in the thirteen colonies at the time leading up to the American Revolution.

The Constitutional model allows free people to worship how, where, or what they may. Religion and churches are available for everyone, according to their own beliefs. People must act responsibly to control government, keep it as an obedient servant, and prevent it from becoming a tyrannical master. Government is to protect the right to worship, the right to speak out, and to provide protection, etc.

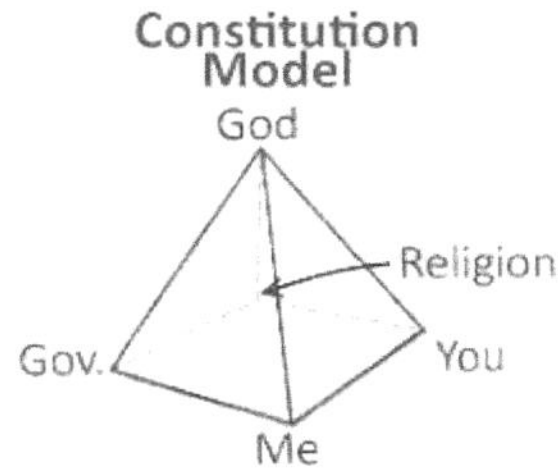

A Constitutional Model

A constitutional model acknowledges the existence and supremacy of God and the inalienable rights of individuals. It provides for a limited and balanced government of, by, and for the people. The purpose of such a constitution is to set up the government, define the government, and to clearly describe the limits of its power.

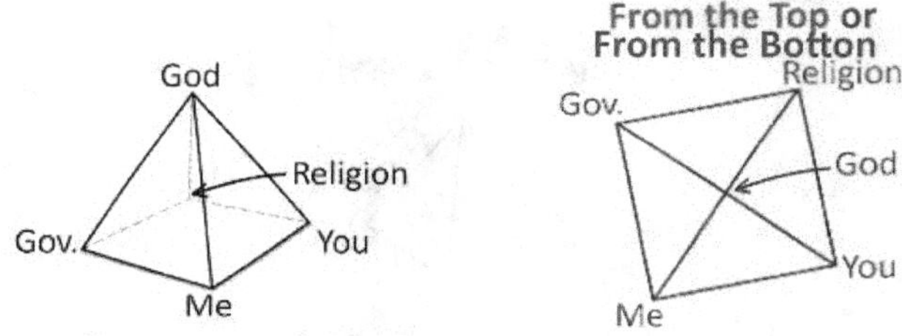

As we examine this constitutional model from the top down or from the bottom up, we see that God is central to everything. God is central to society as a whole. He is central to all religions and is central to the government. If God is lost, we will lose our rights and freedoms, and are left with a government that will ultimately dictate and control. The closer we are to God, the better we can manage government and protect our agency.

1776 and 1787

On July 4, 1776, our Founding Fathers signed the Declaration of Independence to declare their independence from Great Britain. They acknowledged God and divinely given individual rights. They explained the need to separate from Great Britain, their right to throw off tyranny, and their right of self-government. Under this declaration and with divine providence, a great revolution was fought and won.

The Declaration of Independence was inspired of God and created by Patriots who loved liberty. On July 3, 1776, John Adams wrote to his wife, "It may be the will of Heaven that America will suffer calamities still more wasting, and distress yet more dreadful. If this is to be the case, it will have this good effect at least. It will inspire us with many virtues which we have not, and correct many errors, follies and vices which threaten to disturb, dishonor and destroy us. The furnace of affliction produces refinement, in States as well as individuals . . . But I must submit all my hopes and fears to an overruling Providence, in which, unfashionable as the faith may be, I firmly believe."

For a few years after the war, the thirteen colonies celebrated their victory, but they also stumbled to govern themselves. It was at the end of the long, hot summer of 1787 that a Constitutional Convention was organized in Philadelphia, and the Constitution of the United States of America was drafted. There were many disagreements and arguments about issues and concerns of the various new states.

Many compromises had to be made. One concerned votes in Congress for large and small states. Should each state send the same number of delegates to make laws for the country? It was decided that states would elect delegates to the House of Representatives based on population. More populated states would have more delegates, and thus more votes. Delegates to the Senate would be equal, no matter how many people lived in a state. Two senators would be elected from each state. This plan was called the Great **Compromise**.

There was also a great compromise over slavery. It was understood that this issue would need to be settled at a later date. Indeed, it was settled much later by the Civil War. Also, once the Founders started discussing population as a basis for votes in the House of Representatives, the issue of counting slaves became important. Northern states, which had fewer slaves, did not think enslaved people should be counted as part of the population. Southern states, which had many slaves, wanted slaves to count as part of their population so they would get more votes in Congress.

Finally, a compromise was reached. Every five slaves would be counted as three people when figuring out how many representatives a state would send to the House of Representatives. This was the Great Compromise, and allowed the work of writing the Constitution to go on.

United We Stand

By 1790, about three years after it was written, all thirteen states had finally ratified the Constitution of the United States. Two of the founders refused to sign the Constitution because it lacked the language to protect individual rights. Immediately after passage of the Constitution some began working on this and a year later, Congress added the first ten amendments, or Bill of Rights, to the Constitution to protect personal rights.

Every citizen of the United States or any person wanting to become a citizen should become very familiar with the Constitution. They should become familiar with its history and development. Regardless of your religion or your belief in or doubts about God, I invite you to read and ponder the great passages and principles of the Constitution. If we do this as a people, we will be united and strong. The Constitution will become the standard by which we measure issues, proposals, programs, political parties and politicians.

If we as a people hold the Constitution as our standard, we will raise ourselves up out of the noise and confusion of pressing issues and power grabs. We will focus on the things that matter most. We will insist that our candidates and incumbents speak and act accordingly.

A Critical Crossroad

For many recent decades, our country has been stumbling in an effort to discipline itself to act within constitutional limits. We have been approaching this perilous place for some time now. We are now at a critical crossroad in our nation. The nation must choose which path to take.

We the people are again divided. We are not divided by loyalty to a foreign crown or to a specific state. We are not divided over slavery or voting rights. Instead, we are divided over ideologies addressing the increasing role, size, and influence of the federal government. We are divided between depending on God or rejecting Him and depending on people alone.

Remember that God Governs

Our Founding Fathers were so divided during the Constitutional Convention that Benjamin Franklin reminded them that they needed to turn to God for help. It was at the critical moment of success or failure. Franklin said, "God governs in the affairs of men. And if a sparrow cannot fall to the ground without His notice, is it probable that an empire can rise without His aid?" Recorded by James Madison, July 1787

We too must now turn to Him for aid. We must acknowledge Him and our dependence on Him if we are to continue to prosper and to have peace. We can and we must remain one nation under God, indivisible, with liberty and justice for all.

Speech #2

My Personal Decision

Politics

How many times have we thought or heard someone else say: "Politics is a dirty and nasty business. I don't want any part of it." "I don't want to put my family through that mess." "I'm not going to waste my time to vote because one vote doesn't count or make any difference." Or, "All politicians are crooks, and I won't vote for any of them."

Do we realize that these are the thoughts and attitudes that allow bullies and tyrants to gain power and dominance? If we want to maintain freedom, we have to work and fight for it. If we are not willing to do the heavy lifting, we deserve what we get.

Rise to the Occasion

Time and time again great men and women of this blessed land have risen to the occasion in order to fight for and defend freedom, family, and country. The price of liberty has cost the best blood of each generation. The conflict is always about good and evil. The struggle is manifested in a multitude of ways, and victory is always temporary.

Many years ago, the Pilgrims came to America in search of a new life where they could worship God the way they believed was right. Later, when faced with the daunting task of preserving their dreams of freedom from British rule, the Founding Fathers stepped up and did what had to be done and pledged their lives, fortunes, and sacred honor to the cause of freedom. Together they faced the grave possibilities of dishonor, financial ruin, and death if they did not succeed.

Our Daunting Task

Today, understanding the purpose of government has diminished, while demands and expectations of government have increased. Citizens have repeatedly been spoiled, not by defeat, but by prosperity, pride and apathy. Over the past 200 years, the tides of liberty have continued to ebb and flow until we now find the very lifeblood of our nation spilling into the sewers of waste and wantonness.

Once again, we the people of this great nation face the challenge of preserving our freedoms. We need to reacquaint ourselves with the tried and true principles of the U.S. Constitution. We need to step up and make the necessary sacrifices.

Call to Action

This is a call to action. We must search out honest, wise, and good men and women to represent us in public offices. We must run for office ourselves if necessary. We must make a personal pledge of our life, our honor, and our fortune. This is a call to go through the tough times, make the sacrifices and put our families through whatever it takes to preserve our nation. We can do it. Will we do it? That is the question!

Dark Horse Candidate

A "dark horse candidate" is defined in Webster's Dictionary as someone who is a little-known competitor (such as a racehorse) with interesting qualities and unexpected talents or abilities. He is unlikely to succeed and not expected to win, but achieves unexpected support and is nominated during the party convention as a compromise between conflicting factions.

There have been many dark horse candidates in local and state elections. However, there have been only a few for the presidency of the United States, including James K. Polk, Abraham Lincoln, Rutherford Hayes, Warren Harding, and Jimmy Carter. Each was an underdog and nominated by their party, after many ballots, in an effort to bring the people together.

Let Us Begin with the End in Mind

Some time ago, I decided not to run against an incumbent U.S. Congressman, and then later I decided not to run against an incumbent U.S. Senator. Both claimed to be constitutionally grounded, but then voted in Washington like they didn't fully understand the great document that should be the basis for our government. The decisions not to run for those offices were difficult, because I wanted so very much to run and win the campaigns. However, after much prayer, fasting, and consulting with others, I concluded that running for office was not the best path at that time.

I was soon to be retired. My wife and I had always planned to serve others and give back through humanitarian projects, church missions, and political involvement. We decided to serve church missions for the next few years in New York City and then in Italy, or wherever the Lord wanted us.

Halfway through our mission in Harlem I felt an overwhelming need to become more involved in politics. This need began with a stimulating conversation in the barbershop, followed by dynamic impressions, looming thoughts, and pounding ideas. Then there was a two-week period of time during the Christmas holiday season when I was sick with a terrible cough. I had a lot of time to just think and write.

It soon became clear what my wife and I would be doing for the two years following our mission. We would be on the campaign trail. I would run for President of the United States.

We united our faith and began to move forward. Our continued missionary work, however, kept us very busy. When I had a spare hour or two I wrote speeches and planned for the time when we would be released from our mission. The days and weeks passed by very, very quickly. The daunting task seemed overwhelming, but I just had to put my trust in God and move forward one step at a time. That's what I did then, and that's what I'm doing now.

Take One Step at a Time

It is my invitation and challenge to you to also move forward one step at a time to help make dramatic and necessary changes in our government. Read and study the Constitution of the United States of America. As you read it, pray for understanding and to know if it is a divinely inspired document. It will change your thinking and your political perspectives. It is the basis and framework upon which to make all political decisions. America needs you to do this. This is your right and duty.

May God bless you with the wisdom and determination to make a difference the great United States of America.

Speech #3

Announcement and Pledge

Introduction

Today is another great day in the United States of America! It gives me great pleasure to announce to you today, that I am a candidate for President of the United States of America. Many of you don't know me and may not agree with my ideas, but I ask you to give me a chance. I ask you to learn about me and to consider what I will share today and throughout this long campaign.

I come before you this day with confidence that we can do better. I love the United States and its people. I love our national anthem, The Star Spangled Banner. In particular, I would like to recite the words that are part of the fourth verse:

Praise the Power that hath made
and preserved us a nation.
Then conquer we must, when our cause it is just,
And this be our motto: "In God is our trust."

I love the words to the song America the Beautiful:

America! America!
God shed his grace on thee,
And crown thy good, with brotherhood,
From sea to shining sea!

America! America!
God mend thine every flaw,

Confirm thy soul in self-control,
Thy liberty in law!

America! America!
May God thy gold refine;
Till all success be nobleness,
And every gain divine!

May we all sing and shout praises of thanksgiving to:

Our father's God to Thee, Author of liberty,
To Thee we sing.
Long may our land be bright,
with freedom's holy light;
Protect us by Thy might,
Great God, our King!

My Pledge

Today, I pledge to uphold the Constitution and to preserve this great republic. I pledge to do everything I can to resolve the great challenges we face and to strengthen our people, our economy and the rule of law. So that everyone may know, "I pledge allegiance to the Constitution of the United States of America, and to the flag, and to the Republic for which it stands, one nation under God, indivisible, with liberty and justice for all." I will make this pledge of allegiance every day of this campaign and every day that I serve you as President.

I Speak to All

As I speak to all of you today, I acknowledge the God of heaven and earth and pledge to Him and to you my life, my honor, and my meager fortune. I express my gratitude to our Founding

Fathers and to their wives and families. We are grateful to every man, women and child, through the centuries, who fought for the cause of freedom, whatever their sacrifice may have been. To all of them we say, "We love you and we honor you. Thank you so very much. We will pass on to those that follow after us the wonderful legacy of liberty that we have inherited from you."

I speak to those yet unborn. I pledge my best so you can enjoy the benefits of what we will do to protect your rights to life, liberty and the pursuit of happiness, Also, to the billions of people who hope for a better world, I invite you to join with us in thanksgiving. We can all love one another. We can be good neighbors. We can act in good faith to avoid conflict. We can help each other to resolve the problems we face. Let us help one another by personal resolve and commitment, not by government demand.

A Path Less Taken

To all my fellow citizens of these United States and those living in its territories, I invite you to follow me and the other great leaders of this nation on a "path less taken." As you join in this journey, you will experience the same spirit of adventure and excitement that all true patriots feel as they forge ahead for freedom. You will develop a greater love for your fellowman, and you will better lead others to happiness and prosperity while leaving a legacy of liberty. I invite you to give it a try. Let us join our hands together to help each other. Let us firmly lock arms and lift as we move in a steady march forward.

Let Us Doubt Our Doubts Before We Doubt Our Potential

Some people doubt and lose faith before they try to even begin the race. Many worry about things they cannot control.

Let's doubt our doubts before we doubt our potential. Let us have faith, act and move forward as we focus on the things we can control.

Responsibility and Results

Instead of being wasteful or a throwaway society, let's consider an old adage from the Great Depression: "Use it up. Wear it out. Make it do, or do without." There is something good and wholesome about this idea. Something that can help us re-cycle, keep our environment clean, adapt to change, and show respect and gratitude for what we have been given. We've become a throwaway society. Our motto seems to be, "Try it on. Tout it about. Use it once, and then throw it out."

If we are to survive as a country, we must rely on ourselves, not the government. Every home and apartment should have an emergency supply of food, water, and other necessities of life. Some may store rice and beans, while others may prefer flour and preserved fruits and vegetables. With this, you will be able to better financially survive sudden illness or unanticipated unemployment.

Each individual has the freedom to choose. However, anyone who chooses not to plan or take precaution will be responsible for the consequences of their choices. For those who are unable, for whatever reason, I encourage you to look first to your family, then to your church, and then to your neighbors or community. Don't turn to the federal government for welfare payments. To the families, neighbors and communities I encourage you to reach out and open your hearts and your hands to help those in need as much as you can.

National Interests

Likewise, as a nation, we can choose to be wise or foolish. Our government should spend only that which it has. It should encourage every state, city and individual to prepare for difficult times and natural disasters. It is not the Constitutional mandate of the federal government to come to the aid or make whole after storms or earthquakes. It is not the federal government who should bail individuals or companies out of bankruptcy or to make people whole after divorce, unemployment or disaster. That is not the role of the federal government. The federal government should encourage individual, local and state preparation for reparation.

This is not just political rhetoric. I quote President John F. Kennedy who said, "To my fellow Americans, ask not what your country can do for you, but ask what you can do for your country."

I invite you to, "Do unto others as you would have them do unto you."

I invite you and your neighbors, not the federal government, to help take care of each other when necessary.

Let's Go to Work

Let us all together now square our shoulders and lift together wherever we stand. Let us go to work together and get the job done. Let us all work to reduce the national debt and balance the budget. Let us restore to the states their constitutional rights and balance of power. Let us together re-establish reasonable taxation, reasonable immigration, and reasonable legislation.

The PROBLEM: Big Government Is Leading Us to a Welfare State

Some politicians like being the center of attention and argue that they are the only ones who can solve problems. They insist that problems can only be solved their way. They draft more legislation to make more laws requiring more money for more government programs to do more for more people. Then the citizens begin to expect more, and then demand that these politicians do more and more for them.

Part of the problem is the politicians themselves. Part of the problem is all the new legislation and laws created making the problems even bigger. Another part of the problem is that people are forgetting how to solve their own problems and are relying too much on the government to do everything for them.

The SOLUTION: Balance the Budget, Reduce National Debt, and Reduce Government

The main problem of too much spending and not balancing our budget is never really solved. As pundits say, "They just keep kicking the can down the road."

A balanced budget, with reduced federal spending, is the only way to rebuild a robust economy. To achieve and maintain a balanced budget and reduce federal spending we must undertake organizational restructuring. We must curtail spending, and institute economic and welfare reforms. We must reduce the outreach and domination of government.

We Are All Americans

We have many challenges to deal with. We have many problems to solve. The answer is not in how I will do it. The answer is in how we will do it. Together we can do it. We can take courage in the words of others who placed their trust in divine providence.

> *"God knows how we desperately need His guidance and wants to bless us. Whether we are humble or arrogant, rich or poor, free or enslaved, learned or ignorant, loved or forsaken – we can address Him. We need no appointment. He will answer our prayers. We can pray publicly and in private. Fellow Americans, do we think we can rise, grow stronger, and prosper without His help?"*
>
> - Benjamin Franklin

> *"Except the Lord build the House they labor in vain that build it."*
>
> - Psalms 127:1

In his first inaugural address, George Washington declared: "No people can be bound to acknowledge and adore the invisible hand, which conducts the affairs of men, more than the People of the United States. Every step . . . seems to have been distinguished by some token of providential agency."

Abraham Lincoln witnessed that, "I have felt God's hand upon me in great trials and submitted to His guidance, and I trust that as He shall further open the way I will be ready to walk therein, relying on His help and trusting in His . . . wisdom."

Be Assured

Let us all do the same. I want you to know that every day I serve as your President, I will kneel in silent or vocal prayer to give thanks, to ask for guidance, and to pray for all of you and for our nation.

Now, with my wife or alone, I pray for all the leaders of our nation, states and communities. I pray for our military personnel, police officers and fire and emergency responders and their families. I pray for our church's ministers, for our teachers and professors. Especially I pray for the parents and children and families of our nation.

I pray for the leaders and peoples of other nations around the world that they, too, may enjoy God's blessings of peace and prosperity. I pray for our enemies and their families, to soften their hearts that we might be friends.

Let us all now labor together to preserve the Constitution of the United States of America. Let us now pledge together to strengthen our great republic.

Speech #4

Pledge of Allegiance

Greatest Laws

Next to worshipping God, loving our family and being a good neighbor, there is nothing more important than defending the Constitution of the United States. We must put principle above philosophy, party, pocketbook, popularity and personality.

The "Golden Rule" is binding on individuals, organizations and nations. It forbids interference of one with the rights of another. There is nothing in it that is hostile toward good government. Indeed, higher laws support good government.

If we have love, we will not fear. There is liberty in love. Love does not seek to force others, but inspires to do better. Instead, we inspire others to do better. We can extend a hand of friendship and do good to all. By keeping these two great commandments we can truly be free.

Good Versus Evil

There are, and always have been, two opposing forces in the world. They are good and evil. All of us must choose for ourselves which force we will be. Evil, selfishness, and tyranny have always tried to destroy economic, political and religious liberty.

Evil has always advocated absolute security at the sacrifice of freedom. Socialism and communism always promise security. Their promises are attractive and desirable. They try to provide security by different degrees of force, but it is still force. If our desire for security is greater than our desire for liberty, we are doomed.

Satan rages in the hearts of many people. Evil influences are expanding in every segment of our society. They are highly organized, cleverly disguised and powerfully promoted. There are individuals and groups lusting for power, gain and glory. They are in many governments and other organizations. Some seek to overthrow the freedoms of all nations and governments.

Rebellion Against Tyranny

Rebellion against tyranny is a righteous cause, as it was during the American Revolutionary War. Evil forces are fighting for power, domination and control. They are organized in unprecedented ways to attack and mock our prosperity and any faith and religion that does not look exactly like their own.. All of these forces are focusing on destroying us.

Legal vs. Right

We must obey the laws of the land and respect the office and authority of those who serve us. However, it is our responsibility to insure that evil and immorality are not legalized. If evil is legalized, we cannot justify what we do individually, professionally or politically on the basis of what is "legal" rather than on what is "right". If we do, we put at risk our freedom and spiritual foundations. What is legal may be tyrannical or immoral. If we accept this as our standard of conduct, we deny ourselves what is of greatest worth and divine.

The freedoms guaranteed by the U.S. Constitution must not be infringed upon. We are justified in embracing this great document. We, the citizens of this nation, must protect, save and preserve the Constitution by becoming enlightened and abiding by the principles contained therein.

Nature of Government

The nature of government is to expand, exerting more and more influence and power. The nature of patriotism is to control government, keeping its influence and power from invading our privacy and infringing on our rights.

Tyranny is on the march, and we must be a warning voice. If we lose our liberty, we will need to regain it at the price of blood. As conditions worsen, many will call for even more government intervention. We cannot wait for the situation to correct itself. It takes great effort to right the wrongs of tyranny.

We must shrink big government. There is no precedent for even partially dismantling a welfare state in a peaceful and constitutional way. Such a Goliath will not easily submit.

Welfare Entitlements

If we do not recognize the inequalities around us and voluntarily come to the aid of our neighbors, we will be forced to give them aid. Service will be replaced by slavery.

Charity and service must be voluntary. They ennoble both the giver and the receiver. Government efforts to impose charity create more misery and poverty and erode personal liberty. Most of the biggest problems in the world are caused by well-meaning people who ignore the principles of individual freedom. They want to improve life for everyone, so they employ the government to coerce citizens to contribute to massive programs. Millions are forced to give and, in a way, they lose the right to give voluntarily. Those receiving welfare handouts lose their dignity and the desire to live, work or study as they could.

The function of government is to protect life, liberty and property. Anything more than this is illegal and immoral oppression. As government controls, regulations, and taxes increase, they destroy individual rights, personal incentive and potential for reward. Any governmental attempt to redistribute wealth results in the destruction of the productive base of society. Only the ruling elite benefit and enjoy the abundance of their efforts. However, in the end, they too will lose.

Entitlements are a very opressive form of slavery. There are those who honestly desire, through influence of legislation and coercion, to level the world. They do it by stealing from some to giving to others. There is no right way for any individual or government to take by force from one and give to another. This is theft. No matter how many adopt this philosophy and practice, it is still theft. No true patriot would support such programs.

Wealth and property represent labor, industry, intelligence, talent, or inheritance. People can work hard, be innovative, and be wise with how they spend and save their money. Their children can follow their example and build on their inheritance and example and live in abundance. Likewise, others may be lazy, careless, and unwise with how they spend and save their money. Their children, when they grow into adulthood, may follow the examples of their parents and inherit poverty. There is no divine principle or human logic that can justify the poor taking from the pockets of those with more.

The government that robs will want to do more of it. Bondage results when this happens, and all energies, enterprising, and dreaming are crushed in both rich and poor. Those who receive will not appreciate and will soon squander what they have been given. Those who have been robbed will be afraid to again accumulate wealth. They will be forced to hide it or take it elsewhere. Industry and talent will disappear and be replaced by confusion, poverty and ruin.

Individual responsibility and effort is basic to freedom. While there is a great difference in income and property of people here and abroad, it is not the government's job to spread the wealth around the world. Some government efforts and gifts are promoting a culture of dependency.

Responsibility V. Expectation

To give can be noble and to receive can be uplifting, but the right method and mindset of both is vital. A culture of dependency develops where any party becomes dependent on someone else to make decisions or supply resources. It may take many decades, and even generations, to overcome such a culture, but it can be done through personal responsibility.

A culture of personal responsibility lifts all people out of psychological and physical poverty and dependency. Both rich and poor can give and receive with a spirit of thanksgiving. Work, service, and gratitude promote a culture of independence and self-reliance.

Foreign Entitlements

The job of looking after our foreign neighbors is the job of individuals, churches and voluntary organizations. There is nothing in the Constitution that grants the President of the United States or Congress the power to influence the political life of other countries, develop their cultures, stimulate their economies, or to feed their people.

We must first put our own national house in order and solve our own domestic problems before we try to tell others around the world how to live. We should not try to make Americans out of the people of other nations unless they become U.S. citizens. We should not tell our neighbors how to raise their children when we have problems raising our own. If we are hypocrites, we lose all respect and moral authority.

Rough and Tumble of Politics

In every campaign, we hear lots of sweet talk that helps candidates win their elections. But, we are often disappointed because we never see their promises realized. We need candidates who will tell it like it is and who will persuade people to be responsible, instead of focusing on what governement will give or do. It doesn't matter what party a candidate belongs to. What matters is whether he or she understands and upholds the Constitution and sustains its principles.

Political labels change. History repeats itself. We should be tolerant and hold no ill will towards those who do not agree with our views. We should understand, discuss, warn and persuade all citizens to be on the right side of liberty and history. We must be charitable toward all, but be stubborn against evil and tyranny. So come, you who love liberty, and break loose from the oppressor's grasp of excessive govenrment and bureaucracy.

Pledge of Allegiance

My pledge of allegiance is,

"I pledge allegiance to the Constitution of the United States of America, and to the flag and to the Republic for which it stands, one nation under God, indivisible, with liberty and justice for all."

The Constitution, not the flag, is the most important part of our pledge of allegiance.

Speech #5

Friendly Persuasion

Let's Make History Together

Regardless of your circumstances, your past history, weakness or strength, there is room for you in this cause of freedom. You can make a difference in this campaign. Let us make history that will be honorable and inspiring by those who read about us a hundred years from now.

Why Would Anyone Want to Be a Patriot?

Throughout the United States and all around the world, people are crying out for freedom and personal liberty. At a time when political parties and governments are groping for power, citizens everywhere are looking for alternatives. What ideals and principles can they turn to? What kind of government will guarantee their desires?

The principles of patriotism include protecting our divinely given inalienable rights. These rights, as set forth in the first 10 Amendments, are protected by the Constitution of the United States of America.

The Constitution also carefully outlines how to prevent government from controlling the people. It wisely divides the power between the Legislative, Executive, and Judicial Branches, with a provision for each branch to check the others. This "check and balance" system was to prevent any one branch from having all the power.

The Constitution gives limited power to the federal government. The 10th Amendment to the Constitution gives all power not specifically enumerated to be reserved to the states.

Patriotic Benefits

We all share in the "American Dream" to have the opportunity to do and become whatever we want so long as it does not infringe upon the rights of others. We desire to own private property and are promised that the government will protect both our right to property and our property itself. There are many benefits to living in a free land.

To the Tory

The search for true principles has led many people to become Patriots. Some have strayed from these principles and have chosen to accept the ways of a Tory. They now look to the government to solve their problems. They have chosen to use the government to advance a social agenda that takes from producers and gives to the takers. It is sad, but there are those who were once true Patriots, but because of so many influences, they have forgotten and sometimes forsaken patriotic principles.

One might ask, "Why would anyone become a Tory?" Sometimes, we assume it is because the person has gone over to the dark side and wants to destroy freedom and control others. In fact, it is not that simple. Some people have a genuine desire to help those in need, to protect some land or animal species, or have cleaner air or water. The person feels he doesn't have the resources to do alone. So he tries to get the government to force others to get involved. Then it develops into a media campaign to make everyone aware of his concern. This develops into writing

Congressional representatives and insisting that legislation be passed to push through and fund the project.

Unanswered Questions and Mistakes

While waiting in the doctor's office for an appointment, my wife Mary-Jo overheard a man say to the receptionist, "Why should I want to pay for something that someone else will pay for?" She was shocked, and so am I. This is neither honorable nor inspiring.

Patriots and Tories are human and make mistakes. We all have patriotism in our hearts. We all have a little Tory in us too. That doesn't mean we should, or can, allow Tory tendencies to win the day. Each person and each generation must discover for themselves the principles of freedom and how they are to be applied to different issues and situations. There are and will always be differences of opinion. Discussion and debate is vital and healthy.

Good citizens and public servants in all parties and in all states have made mistakes. We all need to re-examine ourselves, our laws, and our policies to evaluate the course we are taking. We can admit our mistakes and make corrections. There is not a U.S. President, a military commander, a legislator, bureaucrat, nor a citizen who has not made a mistake somewhere along the line. We have all made mistakes and we must admit them, learn from them, and correct them.

The Cause of Liberty Needs You

America has a bright future. You can be part of it. America needs you to make history and realize a wonderful destiny. You are needed, and you can make a difference. You don't have to be a problem or even part of the problem. You can be part of the solution. You can act for yourself and help others do the same. Come and add your talents, gifts, and energies to other Patriots. We will all become better as a result.

It is natural to have questions and to begin thinking about answers. The government is not the answer. You are the answer. Your neighbor is the answer.

Come, Join with Me!

America needs you! The Statue of Liberty says, "Give me your tired, your poor, your huddled masses yearning to breathe free, the wretched refuse of your teeming shore. Send these, the homeless, tempest-tossed to me, I lift my lamp beside the golden door."

To all new immigrants, I say, America needs you. But, when you come, you must come to be an American. Come to be a Patriot and not a Tory. Come to be independent and not dependent on the government. Come here to succeed.

Let's Be Patriots

Regardless of our occupation, race, religion, age, or gender, we all have experienced failure. And, we have all experienced success and will succeed in the future. It is important that we succeed in the right things. My father always said, "Be careful of what you want because you will probably get it." We must succeed in the cause of liberty and not in government control. Regardless of who we are, we are brothers and sisters on this planet. We can work together in the cause of freedom and civilization.

The whole world is watching to see what the United States will do and how we will solve our problems. Our freedom and the freedom of others depends on our choices and whether we are Patriots or Tories. Let us be Patriots.

Speech #6

Constitutional President v. Bully President

Constitutional Intent

The Constitution of the United States intended to limit the power and influence of the President so that no person or one party could become too powerful. The Founding Fathers and other Patriot citizens wanted to move as far away from a monarchy as they could to insure that nobility and dictatorship could never get rooted in the American political system.

Constitutional President

There was a time when the President was the key watchdog, making sure the federal government was going its job. The President's efforts were used to promote the Constitutional agenda and restrain the other branches from doing foolish things.

The earlier presidents all saw this office as one of duty and difficulty. George Washington admitted that he, "was beset by 'unmerited censures' of the vilest kind."

Thomas Jefferson described the presidency as "a splendid misery."

Andrew Jackson complained that the job of being president was "a situation of dignified slavery."

With few exceptions, most presidents before and during the Civil War stayed within the bounds of their Constitutional constraints. Abraham Lincoln acted within the bounds of

Constitutional authority in order to preserve the Union. However, almost every president that followed him realized that public opinion and their office allowed them to stretch their authority beyond what had ever been done before.

Straying from the Path

Many presidents began to take just a few steps off the prescribed Constitutional path. The many political parties dwindled to two. Perhaps they wanted to be like the powerful and dynamic industrial tycoons and leaders of the time. The public became accustomed to more and more powerful executives and watched in anticipation of what their new president would try to do.

Some complained that they were being restrained from doing what needed to be done for the good of the country. James A. Garfield asked, "What is there in this place that a man should ever want to get in to it?"

From 1901-1909, Theodore Roosevelt became famous for using his office as a "bully pulpit" to get his way. Just a few years later, in 1913, Woodrow Wilson set in motion a multitude of things that would dramatically take America off the constitutional course it had struggled so hard to stay on for over a hundred years. In 1921, Warren G. Harding complained to the nation that "this White House is a prison." Herbert Hoover persuaded the public into feeling that the President needed more power when he described the office as "a compound hell."

Rise of Corporate CEOs

Both Republican and Democrat presidents were trying to make their mark in history. The only way to do that was to differentiate themselves in achievement, bullying, or change—the ABCs of politics. Corporations flourished and began to grow and dominate the marketplace and economic landscape. Multitudes of shareholders voted to elect a board of directors to select their presidents and vice presidents to grow their company and make them a profit.

The rise of these corporate CEOs (Chief Operating Officers) fascinated the public mind and became the models of success. Students began to study, apprentice, and develop their resumes in order to climb the corporate ladder so they could rise as high and as fast as possible. Many things changed the business and social dynamics.

Rise of Professional Politicians

Almost simultaneously, fewer and fewer statesmen were being chosen by popular support. Those with ambition and desire to serve recognized that they needed to be either a person of wealth and intellect, or a war hero. Many began preparing themselves by beginning their "political careers" in local or state offices and working their way up the political ladder in hopes that someday they would get a shot at running for the White House.

In this process of immersing themselves in the waves of public opinion and the tides of opportunistic compromise, so many have been lost at sea and forgotten their bearings of Constitutional principles. Government is no longer of, by, and for the people. Public officials and employees have become an industry in, of, and to themselves.

The most dramatic abuse of power is with the office of President. Everyone from both parties seems to have abused power beyond their Constitutional limits. Each justifies their actions and/or ignores criticism, but almost all of them are guilty of this abuse. This abuse has increased with each President and is escalating in degree and intent.

Electing the Best Bully to Be President

Each election, candidates from both parties try to win the "beauty contest" of who is more attractive to the majority of voters. Little consideration is ever given, discussed, or required as to the discipline or constraint these candidates have shown in staying within the bounds of their authority. Each boasts of a "resume" summarizing their ability to bully their opponents.

The American public has become enamored with winners. They always want to see a good fight. Unless someone is willing to "duke it out" they are considered weak. Too many people like to hear strong, bold words and dramatic expressions. Too few respond to reason, logic, and respect.

Too often, the character of candidates for the House and the Senate is measured not on integrity or loyalty to the Constitution, but to their ability to debate and intimidate. Their accomplishments are measured only by what they have taken from others and given to their district or state. Instead of going to Washington, D.C., to promote the general welfare, they go with the intent to get everything they can from the pockets of others and bring it back to their constituents. They call it "pork" or "bringing home the bacon." The saddest thing is that too many constituents expect this of their public servants. Eventually, one of these political gladiators becomes President of the country and charges off to do something greater than the last president.

America Needs a Real Constitutional President

America needs a President who is taking care of business here in the United States. The President is elected to work full-time in order to execute the law and insure that he and the other branches of government are serving the people within the guidelines of the Constitution.

The President should be granted reasonable times for vacations, but not unlimited time, and family vacations should be paid for out of his salary. Reasonable advertising should be permitted, but non-stop travel for self-promotion or supporting other candidates is not in the job description of the President. This behavior has become accepted behavior, but is a serious problem in our political system.

A bully president spends time trying to push a personal or party agenda regardless of Constitutional constraints. The agenda should be upholding, protecting, and following the Constitution. A real Constitutional President governs and serves the people. America needs and deserves this.

Speech #7

Freedom of Religion and Speech

Bill of Rights – Amendment 1

"Congress shall make no law respecting an establishment of religion, or prohibiting the free exercise thereof; or abridging the freedom of speech, or of the press; or the right of the people peaceably to assemble, and to petition the government for a redress of grievances."

Rights Come with Responsibilities

The Founding Fathers deliberately provided two guarantees for the protection of religious freedom. It is always important to remember and defend the rights of religious worship and free speech that are protected by the Constitution. They are the foundation of our nation, and we have reason to be concerned about their preservation. However, the best way to do this is to speak of them in gratitude and not by way of demand. We are grateful for these cherished and protected rights, but our requirement should be in living up to the responsibilities they represent.

We cannot speak of religious worship without free speech. We should worship God and allow others to worship how, where or what they may. We should speak of truth and of what we think is good, and allow others to do the same without ridicule or intimidation.

Religious speech has priority over other types of speech because it is fundamental to the free exercise of religion.

Religious worship and discussion are forms of speech. Each strengthens the other. I am concerned that religious values, voices and motivations are being marginalized to the point of censorship or condemnation. They are being labeled as off-limits in public discussion or law making. This labeling of religious worship is being applied selectively by its opponents.

Religious Freedom

In exercising our religious freedom and preventing the government from intruding, we need to find a balance in upholding this part of the First Amendment. Concerns over this issue were expressed by the Danbury, Connecticut, Baptists in their letter to the President dated October 7, 1801. Thomas Jefferson responded and reassured them in his letter dated January 1, 1802, that they had no need to fear because of the "wall of separation between Church and State."

There are some today who proclaim that this wall was built to keep religion out of government and the public forum. In supporting this idea, they begin to discount and avoid their personal and social responsibilities. In supporting this logic, they abdicate a great portion of the rights afforded them by the Bill of Rights. At the same time, they propose state power over God's supremacy. Once this is done, it is the beginning of the end to religious freedom, but there is no end to state control.

Free Speech

Freedom of speech is being diminished in private discussion and public debate. There is a chilling effect of invisible restraints and censorship of unpopular views and unwelcome facts. This is manifested in most media, professional journals and academic employment decisions. It is bolstered by enforcing political correctness and organized restraints to punish specific individuals and messages.

This should never be an issue in America. It was an issue in pre-World War II Germany and many other countries who fell to dictators. The very fact that it is a concern today is alarming in and of itself. The same thing is beginning to happen here that happened there. We see new laws criminalizing "hate speech" and expanded government intervention to target communications. We see scholars being unable to publish, or being punished for writing unfavorable material. We see schools, universities and accrediting associations focused on promoting political correctness. We see campus speech codes, boycotts, firings and intimidation to suppress and make illegal personal expression. These are improper infringements on free speech.

It is appropriate and vital to hear all voices in a free society. The proper response to free speech that a person or group disagrees with is to respond with their own speech. There should never be any attempt to coerce or silence an opponent.

Taking Religious Offense

Demeaning religious worship is becoming more common these days. Taking personal or religious offense and then lashing out with violence is not the solution to offensive insults. It is appropriate and necessary to be firm, but wise and understanding. There is an old saying, "It is easier to make friends than to make laws." Seeking mutual understanding and toning down the loud public rhetoric is the appropriate approach to such situations. Freedom is weakened by legal remedies against insult.

A much larger threat to free exercise of religion is federal and state actions and court decisions that attempt to subordinate exercise of religion to "civil rights". No federal anti-discrimination legislation should try to trump the First Amendment's right to freedom of religion, speech, press, assembly, and petition. It does not similarly apply to demands of abortion, employment, and same-sex marriage. Laws can and should be based on moral principle.

Public Debate and Religious Opinion

Public debate must include religious opinion as well as public reason. One should not and cannot exclude the other from policy debates or law making. Religion is both a private and a public matter protected by the First Amendment. The framers of the Constitution never intended that public reason would crowd out religious voices and values. Public debate and religious opinion are the very basis for legal and policy argument on public issues and citizen referenda or legislative law making.

True and pure religious insights, values and motives are just as important today as they were 50 or 200 years ago. It is vital that religious belief be part of our public discourse and have equal access to the public square. This was the case with the abolition of slavery and the Civil Rights movement. Society benefits from religious light, knowledge, and wisdom because people feel accountable to God.

Stereotyping

Even some religious speech is being labeled as irrational, bigoted and promoting hatred. This diminishes and jeopardizes both freedom of religion and speech and has a chilling effect on public debate. The Supreme Court held, "If there is any fixed star in our constitutional constellation, it is that no official, high or petty, can prescribe what shall be orthodox in politics, nationalism, religion, or other matters of opinion, or force citizens to confess by word or act their faith therein."

- West Virginia Board of Education v. Barnette

Denying a person, church or religious organization the right of access to federal courts would be repeating what happened in the Dred Scott case of 1857. The Supreme Court ruled that a black person had no access to the federal courts. It polarized the nation and helped to precipitate the country toward civil war. We need not learn this lesson twice.

Unwritten and Unenforced Laws

We respect the rule of law. This means that no government leader can rule by whim or edict. Government leaders must rule by the laws created by both houses of the Legislative Branch, signed by the Executive Branch, and interpreted by the Judicial Branch of our government. The government is not above the law. The President is not above the law. Our government system is based on law.

However, we must remember that society is not primarily held together by law and its enforcement. We are held together by our willingness to voluntarily obey the unenforceable laws of being good and behaving correctly. Some call these psychological agreements. Regardless, belief in right and wrong is fundamental to motivating our large population to voluntarily comply with social courtesy and harmony. Patience and goodwill will generate respectful co-existence and synergy. The important decisions will not be in the courts, but in our hearts.

Speech #8

Legitimate Legislation

Bills and Laws Must Be Understandable

Let no bills be signed into law that are cannot be read and understood by the "reasonable" person. Bills should rarely be longer that the U.S. Constitution itself. Each legislator should read and understand the bill before debating it and voting on it. This can easily be determined by their declaration in good faith, along with a brief quiz that each legislator can perform prior to presenting it before the floor for debate and vote.

The bills and the results of such examination should be part of the public Congressional Record. Public servants should be held responsible for what they do and what they support. Both federal and state legislation and voting should be reported and available to the public.

Free to Choose

God has given us specific inalienable rights. The U.S. Constitution guarantees the protection of some of these rights. It reserves to the people the right to create a government based on the rule of law. It also established and clearly defines how proposed laws are to be considered, approved and signed into law. When such proposals are properly brought forth and approved, we have legitimate laws that are binding upon everyone in the United States.

We are free to create and obey constitutional law and live in freedom. If we create unconstitutional or illegitimate laws, we forfeit some of our freedom and have to live with the consequences. Some illegitimate laws may have parts that are good, but if it is not constitutional in its entirety, it should and must be rejected in its entirety or rewritten and approved by both houses and the President.

In their wisdom, our Founding Fathers provided a check and balance system so ill-conceived and illegitimately passed laws could be negated. If, in their opinions, the justices of the Supreme Court find parts of the law that are legitimate and constitutional, they can comment and thus guide the legislative and the executive branches in the future. However, if the law is not constitutional in its entirety, it must be struck down in its entirety so Congress can begin again. Otherwise you have the Supreme Court creating laws a la carte. This is neither legitimate nor constitutional law making.

Illegitimate Law

It is what I call the "illegitimate law" I wish to address here. It may be good. It may be constitutional. But if citizens can't understand the law and lawmakers don't know how to enforce the law, I suggest that it is illegitimate, and therefore unconstitutional.

No One Read It!

I will use one well-known and currently controversial law as my example. I will use the Affordable Care Act (ACA). It may be a good idea, but I don't know because I haven't read it. I don't think anyone read it before voting for or against it or signing it into law.

The Speaker of the House of Representatives at the time, said to pass it and then find out what's in it. She didn't read it.

The Republicans didn't read it either. They opposed it because the Democrats proposed it. Maybe some of their staff members read some of it, but no one read all 2,000 + pages and really understood what was in it. No Senator or Representative read the whole bill or understood it in its entirety before they voted for its passage.

The bill contained amendments that had nothing to do with heath care. Thus, the bill is clearly illegitimate, and there may be parts of this bill that are clearly unconstitutional. Who knows? No one knows because no one has read it or understands it in its entirety. President Obama wanted it passed, and he signed it into law. He didn't read it either! When does the President or legislators have time to read a 2000-plus-page book?

No one in the press read it either, including those who call themselves conservative watchdogs. They viciously snarled and barked warnings that something bad was happening. None of them read it either. When do they have time? If they had read it, they would have been informed. They expected their producers and staff to do their homework, but no one did it.

The government tennis match volleyed back and forth. The press worked up the frenzy as they watched it happen. The public spectators ended up wondering what happened. No one read it! We argue and debate and no one knows what they are talking about. It may be good, or some parts may be good, but it's illegitimate and should be rejected on this basis.

Presidential Promise

When I am elected President of the United States, I will veto any bill that does not pass the "Certified Simple Test." There are three parts to this test:

1. length
2. understanding
3. legitimacy

I will veto any legislation that is longer than the U.S. Constitution. This is the test of length.

I will veto any bill that parents, teachers, and students cannot read, understand, and discuss. This is the test of understanding.

I will veto any bill that has not been read by every member of the House and the Senate who votes on it. I will demand that their vote signifies that they have read it, or I will veto it. This is the legitimacy part of the test.

The public must hold their public servants accountable to do their homework and be honest in how they do it. If legislators don't do their homework, they should flunk, be suspended or expelled. If we do not demand this, we deserve what we get. Heaven help us if there is ever another Constitutional Convention. We will end up with a 10-volume edition of a new constitution that no one will read or understand.

Work Enough to Do

We can't just complain about government and laws. Any president or lawmaker who will not, or cannot, deliver on a promise to read and understand bills for proposed laws before they vote or sign must and will be held accountable before the people of the United States of America. We have work to do, so let's get out and do it!

Speech #9

Relocating Our Capital City

Washington, D.C.

Article 1, Section 8.17 of the U.S. Constitution permits the establishment of a district not to exceed 10 miles square that will serve as the nation's seat of government by cession of state land and acceptance of Congress. It was intended that the federal government capital provide for its own maintenance and security.

Under the Constitution, the first capital, New York City, was on the Hudson River in the North. Then the Residence Act of 1790 approved the creation of the nation's capital on the Potomac River in the South. President George Washington was to select 100 square miles of land for a district that would not be part of any state. At the time the land was part of Virginia on one side of the Potomac, and Maryland on the other. To compensate these states for their land, the federal government agreed to pay their remaining war debts from the Revolutionary War.

Washington hired Benjamin Banneker to help lay out a city that would be the seat of the federal government. On September 9, 1791, the city was called Washington, in honor of President Washington. The federal district was named Columbia, which was a poetic name for the United States commonly in use at that time. Congress held its first session in Washington on November 17, 1800.

Over time, due to lack of funds to pay for its upkeep, the city disintegrated. In 1873, following the Civil War, large-scale projects were started in order to modernize the city. However, they bankrupted the District's government. Many years later, following the New Deal in the 1930's, increased federal spending created new buildings, memorials and museums. World War II increased the number of federal employees working in the District.

Over the years, the financial capital of the country migrated from New York City to the legal capital of Washington, D.C. An explosive growth in special interests, lobbyists and law offices dramatically changed the political environment inside and outside the capital. It was a place of turmoil during Civil Rights marches, and on September 11, 2001, an airplane piloted by foreign terrorists crashed into the Pentagon. Such change and turmoil have caused concern for the integrity, efficiency and safety of the nation's capital.

New Seat of Government

In our current economic distress and political turmoil, we need a new vision for our country. Part of that vision needs to include a new location to house our seat of government. Expansive population and tourism growth, along with tremendous traffic congestion, increases the threat from land, sea or air. It is quite obvious that the location of Washington, D.C., has many disadvantages and is vulnerable to a multitude of threats. It isn't if, but when, these disadvantages will overcome the capital as now located.

While the District of Columbia will always remain a monument to the past 200 years, the future capital must provide for increased efficiency and safety. Such a location must consider all aspects of a modern capital including resources, transportation systems and the surrounding area.

Liberty, Missouri

The two most ideal locations would be immediately east of Liberty, Missouri, or adjacent to Whitman Air Force Base between Warrensburg and Sedalia, Missouri. This ten-square mile district would have a surrounding buffer zone and provide state-of-the-art work facilities, housing, and transportation for only the top officials in the three branches of governments. All staff, foreign diplomats and other parties would be required to be located off-site.

The country's original capital in Philadelphia was moved many times. It was moved to New York City. Then it was moved back to Philadelphia for about ten years, and then to Washington, D.C. The place was chosen in part to be in the middle of the country and have access to foreign ports.

It is now long past the time for our capital to be moved to the heartland of America. The costs and immediate inconvenience will be far outweighed by the benefits and savings. There may be some controversy about the exact location in Missouri, but there can be no justifiable rational for not having the kind of capital we need at this time in history.

Speech #10

The United Nations

Why the United Nations?

There is no justification or advantage for the United States to be involved in the United Nations. There is very little to gain and much to lose. The United States gives foreign aid to have other governments finance their U.N. representatives to come and live in the U.S. and promote the U.N. agenda. The U.N. entangles our foreign diplomats and military forces in projects and offensives that we have no business being involved in.

The United Nations charter has not turned out to be a charter of peace. Instead, it is a charter fostering turmoil around the world and of undermining the sovereignty of the United States. Its intent is to have growing global influence and control and dominion over the U.S. and other nations. Although it appears to have many good intentions, it is very ineffective accomplishing these goals and uses them to front other major initiatives. It is a forum for many individuals and organizations to weaken the strength of our republic and undermine our national security. Urgent measures need to be made to:

- Stop funding the United Nations.
- Move the U.N. headquarters outside of the United States of America.
- Eliminate diplomatic privilege and immunity to U.N. members, staff and their dependents.
- Withdraw as a member of the U.N.

United Nations Charter

"The Charter of the United Nations was signed on 26 June 1945, in San Francisco, at the conclusion of the United Nations Conference on International Organization, and came into force on 24 October 1945. The Statute of the International Court of Justice is an integral part of the Charter." Introductory Note for U.N. Charter

Like so many Americans, I grew up thinking that the United Nations was a noble organization of charity, reason and good will. The first time I saw the United Nations building and flags I thought how wonderful it is that we can all work together to help one another. On the surface, this has been the image of the United Nations for many years, but upon reading the U.N. Charter and comparing what the U.N. is doing around the world, what the U.N. does and wants to do is much, much more.

Perception and Reality

There are many noble causes that are promoted and supported by the U.N. Most of those affiliated with the U.N. are convinced that there are only altruistic motives for working together to feed the hungry, provide medical aid to the sick, clothes and housing to the poor and support and encouragement to those being bullied or terrorized. This perception is more of a promotion than the resulting reality.

The U.N. Charter advocates good ideas and peaceful ends, but instead is an ideology and a map leading to world domination. Instead of a charter of peace, it is a charter of war. Since its inception, there has been constant conflict and methodic maneuvering. This suggested forum for peaceful discussion and search for solutions is actually an arena to entangle and weaken selective participants.

Almost immediately following the defeat of Germany in April and early May of 1945, the United Nations was established in San Francisco. President Truman signed the treaty in hopes that the U.N. would serve as an arbiter of international disputes before they got out of hand. In August of 1945, two Atomic bombs were dropped on Japan, and the war ended.

All members are now bound by the articles of this treaty obligating them to the U.N. over all other treaty obligations. Most countries in the world have now ratified the Charter. From serving as an arbiter, the U.N. has evolved and emerged as a pseudo world governing organization. Instead of securing a path to peace, there has been a trail of conflict and war. Instead of arbitrating disputes, the U.N. arbitrarily manipulates conflicts to its own advantage.

Question of Sovereignty

It is one thing to work together with allies in the theater of war against world aggression. But, it is a very different thing to have U.S. soldiers serve under the United Nations flag and under foreign commanders. The very notion of a one-world government with a worldwide military strikes at the heart of our national sovereignty. There are resolutions being discussed and passed that are attempting to control America's food supply, fuel production, military capabilities and the right to bear arms.

U.N. Out of U.S. and U.S. Out of U.N.

The United States has little to gain and much to lose in its association with the U.N. The United Nations should be moved out of the United States and the United States must get out of the United Nation.

Speech #11

Governing Principles

Patriotic principles are founded on higher laws. They are founded on the laws of God. These laws are called commandments. Commandments are guidelines to help us avoid problems and achieve success.

Commandments to Live By

The greatest commandment, as given in the Bible in Matthew 22:36-40 says: ". . . which is the great commandment in the law? Jesus said unto him, Thou shalt love the Lord thy God with all thy heart, and with all thy soul, and with all thy mind. This is the first and great commandment. And the second is like unto it, Thou shalt love thy neighbor as thyself. On these two commandments hang all the law . . ."

A lesser law was given to Moses on Mount Sinai, **where God gave** the Ten Commandments to the Israelites. This is recorded in the Bible in **Exodus 20:3-17.**

1. Thou shall have no other gods before me.
2. Thou shall not make for yourself any graven image.
3. Thou shall not take the name of the Lord thy God in vain.
4. Remember the Sabbath day, to keep it holy.
5. Honor thy father and thy mother.
6. Thou shall not murder.
7. Thou shall not commit adultery.
8. Thou shall not steal.
9. Thou shall not bear false witness against thy neighbor.
10. Thou shall not covet.

Laws to Govern By

The following are ten laws of wise governing:

1. Governments are instituted of God for the benefit of society and to hold individuals and groups accountable for their acts, both in making and administering laws for the good and safety of society.
2. Governments have the right to enact laws to secure the public interest while protecting freedom of conscience, the right to control property, and protect life.
3. Civil officers are needed to enforce law and administer justice in upholding the voice of the people.
4. Citizens are bound to sustain and uphold the government protecting them, uphold the laws of the land, and should be punished for crimes.
5. Crimes should be punished according to the nature of the offense.
6. Governments must protect freedom to exercise religious belief so long as a regard and reverence are shown to the laws and such religious opinions do not justify sedition nor conspiracy.
7. Citizens should be tolerant of those who are different, and treat one another with respect and courtesy.
8. Citizens should appeal to civil law for redress of wrongs. However, they are justified in defending themselves, their friends and property and the government from unlawful assaults and encroachments where immediate appeal cannot be made to laws and relief afforded.
9. Government should not interfere in foreign countries, acknowledging that their policies and customs are different from ours.
10. Citizens should seek out and support honest, wise, and good men for public office.

Dangers to Avoid

Thomas Jefferson warned, "Power tends to corrupt and absolute power corrupts absolutely . . . Single acts of tyranny may be ascribed to the accidental opinion of a day; but a series of oppressions, begun at a distinguished period, and pursued unalterably through every change of ministers, too plainly prove a deliberate systematical plan of reducing us to slavery."

George Washington also warned, "Government is not reason, it is not eloquence – it is force. Like fire, it is a dangerous servant and a fearful master."

Declaration of Independence

The Declaration of Independence affirms that:

1. There are times when it is justified to separate a people and form a new nation.
2. All men are created equal and endowed with unalienable rights of life, liberty and the pursuit of happiness.
3. Governments derive their powers from the consent of the people.
4. When any form of government becomes destructive to these ends, it is the right of the people to alter or abolish it and institute new government with a foundation of principles of safety, happiness and prudence.

Long-standing governments should not be changed for light or transient causes. When a long history of abuses occur, however, it is the people's right, and their duty, to throw off such government, and to provide new government for their future security and well-being.

The Constitution of the United

The following is a brief summation of the Constitution:

Preamble

The Constitution was created in order to form a more perfect Union, establish Justice, insure domestic Tranquility, provide for the common Defense, promote the general Welfare, and secure the Blessings of Liberty to ourselves and to our posterity.

Article I

The Legislative Branch is formed with all legislative powers (power to make laws for the entire country) are vested in a Congress consisting of a Senate and House of Representatives.

The members of the House of Representatives are elected every two years by voters in each state. The number of Representatives for each state is based on the population of each state.

Each state elects two Senators, who serve a term of six years.

Article II

The Executive Branch is formed with the executive power vested in a President of the United States for a four-year term, together with a Vice President chosen for the same term. Both are elected by electors, appointed by each state, equal to the total number of the Representatives and Senators from that state. The person who received the highest number of votes was elected as president, and the person who received the next-highest number of votes was elected as vice-president. (This was later changed by the 12th Amendment.)

The President may appoint a Cabinet of advisors. The President has the power to execute, or carry out, the laws of the country. Powers granted to the President are:

- To be Commander in Chief of the Army and Navy, and of the militia of the states when called into service of the United States.
- To pardon, or free, people convicted of federal crimes
- To make treaties, but they must be approved by two-thirds of the Senate.
- To name ambassadors, important government officials, and judges of the Supreme Court and other federal courts, with the approval of the Senate.

The duties of the President include informing Congress from time to time on the condition of the nation. Today, the President does this in a State of the Union address once a year.

Article III

The Judicial Branch has judicial power vested in a Supreme Court, and inferior courts as Congress may establish. Supreme Court and other federal judges hold office for life if they "act properly."

Among other powers, Federal Courts have legal authority over all laws made under the Constitution, treaties made with foreign governments, cases involving the federal government, cases involving different states or citizens of different states, and cases involving foreign citizens or government. Federal Courts do not judge criminal cases;

criminal cases are tried in the state where the crime took place.

Article IV

Relations among the states. Gives full faith and credit to public acts, records and judicial proceedings of all states. Citizens of each state are entitled to all U.S. privileges and immunities. Charged criminals are to be extradited to the state of crime scene. New states may be admitted to the Union by Congress, but not by division or combination of states or parts of states without consent of state legislatures and Congress. Congress can dispose of and regulate U.S. property. The United States guarantees all states a republican form of government, and protects states against invasion and domestic violence when applied for by a state legislature.

Article V

Amending the Constitution. There are two ways to make amendments, or changes, to the Constitution: two-thirds (2/3) vote of each branch of Congress can suggest an amendment; or, two-thirds of the state legislatures can call a convention to suggest an amendment. Then three-fourths (¾) of the state legislatures or state conventions must approve the amendment.

Article VI

Debt, Federal Supremacy, Oaths of Office. The United States government promises to pay back all debts and honor all agreements made by previous governments. The Constitution is the supreme law of the land and all judges and state laws are bound by it. Senators, Representatives, Executive and Judicial Officers of the U.S. and the states shall be bound by oath to support this Constitution. No religious test shall ever be required as a qualification for a person to hold a federal office.

Article VII

Ratification of the Constitution would be required of at least 9 of the 13 original states.

The Bill of Rights: the First 10 Amendments, 1791

By 1790, about three years after it was written, all thirteen states had finally ratified the Constitution of the United States. Two of the founders refused to sign the Constitution because it lacked the language to protect individual rights. So, immediately after passage of the Constitution some began working on this and a year later, Congress added the first ten amendments, or Bill of Rights, to the Constitution to protect personal rights.

Initially, five states—Delaware, Pennsylvania, New Jersey, Georgia, and Connecticut—were the first to ratify the Constitution. Then some states expressed their concern that the document did not contain a Bill of Rights. They wanted a document stating that the government could not take away the rights that were listed in the Declaration of Independence. John Hancock, then governor of Massachusetts, persuaded the delegates that such a bill of rights could be added as amendments to the Constitution after the document was ratified. Following his advice, by 1789, nine states had ratified the document.

By the next year, in 1790, all 13 states had ratified it. A year later, in 1791, (three years after the Constitution was written) Congress added the first Ten Amendments to the Constitution—known as the Bill of Rights.

Amendment 1.

Freedom of religion, speech, press, peaceable assembly and to petition the government for a redress of grievances.

Amendment 2.

Right to Keep Weapons. State militia and right to keep and bear arms.

Amendment 3.

Protection against Quartering Soldiers. No soldiers shall be quartered in any house without the owner's consent, but as prescribed by law.

Amendment 4.

Freedom from Unreasonable Searches and Seizures. No warrants without probable cause, supported by oath or affirmation, and description of place, persons or things to be seized.

Amendment 5.

Rights of Persons Accused of a Crime. Grand jury indictment for capital crime, except in military, war or public danger. No double jeopardy or being compelled to witness against self. Due process of law and compensation for condemnation.

Amendment 6.

Right to a Jury Trial in Criminal Cases. Right to a speedy and public trial by an impartial jury. To be informed of the accusation and confronted with witnesses against the accused. To have defense counsel.

Amendment 7.

Rights to a Jury Trial in Civil Cases. In suits at common law, where the value in controversy shall exceed twenty dollars, the right of trial by jury shall be preserved.

Amendment 8.

Protection from Unfair Fines and Punishment. No excessive bail, fines nor cruel and unusual punishment.

Amendment 9.

Other Rights of the People. People have additional rights not stated in the Constitution.

Amendment 10.

Powers of the States and the People. The powers not granted to the United States by the Constitution, and not forbidden to the states, are reserved to the states or to the people.

Additional Amendments

Starting in 1798, more amendments were added to the Constitution. The last was added in 1992.

Amendment 11.

Limiting Law Cases against States (1798).

A state government cannot be sued in a federal court by people of another state, or by people from a foreign country.

Amendment 12.

Election of President and Vice President (1804).

This amendment changed the method of choosing a President and Vice President. In an electoral college, Electors meet in their states and vote for President and Vice President, who now run together. The team who receives more than half the electoral votes in elected.

Amendment 13.

Slavery Outlawed (1865).

Neither slavery nor involuntary servitude, except as punishment for a convicted criminal, shall exist in the United States.

Amendment 14.

Rights of Citizens (1968).

All persons born or naturalized in the U.S. are citizens of the U.S. and of the state wherein they reside. States cannot abridge privileges or immunities of U.S. citizens; nor can they deprive any person of life, liberty, or property, without due process of law and equal protection of the laws.

Representatives shall be apportioned according to their respective numbers, counting all the people in each State, excluding Indians not taxed. (This was later repealed.) Apportionment increases or decreases according to the number of male voters. (This section aimed to force states in the South to allow African Americans to vote, which many were preventing at the time.)

No person shall hold high public office if they have engaged in insurrection, rebellion or aids enemies unless Congress removes such disability.

All money borrowed by the U.S. government to fight the Civil War is to be repaid, no debts owed to the Confederate states to pay for their expenses in the war are to be paid back by the federal or state governments. No money would be paid for the loss of people they once held in slavery.

Amendment 15.

Voting Rights (1870).

Gave the right to vote regardless of race, color, or previous condition of servitude. This amendment was aimed to give black men the right to vote, and did not address women's voting rights.

Amendment 16.

Income Tax (1913)

Gave Congress the power to collect income tax directly from individuals. This amendment opened the door to taxation without limitation and NEEDS TO BE REPEALED!

Amendment 17.

Direct Election of Senators (1913).

Senators would be elected directly by the people instead of by the State legislatures as they were previously. This amendment takes power away from the state government and NEEDS TO BE REPEALED!

Amendment 18.

Prohibition of Alcoholic Drinks (1919).

Prohibited the making, selling or transporting of alcoholic drinks in the United States. This bad law that gave more power to the government was later repealed.

Amendment 19.

Women's Right to Vote (1920).

Voting rights could not be denied on account of sex. Women's right to vote was long overdue and gave power to the people.

Amendment 20.

Terms of Office (1933)

Terms of President and Vice President shall begin at noon on January 20. The terms for Senators and Representatives begin at noon on January 3rd.

Congress shall assemble at least once in every year, beginning at noon January 3.

If the President dies before taking office, the Vice President elect shall become President.

In some situations such as death or being unqualified,

Congress may pass a law determining how to choose the President and Vice President.

Amendment 21.

Repeal of Prohibition (1933).

Repealed Amendment 18.

Amendment 22.

President Limited to Two Terms (1951).

The President can only be elected for two terms. This rule must be kept!

Amendment 23.

Presidential Elections for the District of Columbia (1961).

Citizens living in the District of Columbia shall appoint a number of electors equal to the number of Senators and Representatives to which the District would be entitled if it were a state, but no more than the least populous state. This is important because people living the District have no state legislature, and thus were previously unable to vote for the President.

Amendment 24.

Poll Tax Ended (1964).

No person can be prevented from voting in a federal election for failing to pay a poll tax or any other kind of tax.

Amendment 25.

Presidential Succession (1967).

This sets forth procedures of replacing the President or Vice President in the event of death, resignation, or incapacity. In part, the amendment says:

The Vice President becomes President on the death or resignation of the President.

If the Vice President dies or resigns, the President nominates a replacement, who takes office when confirmed by majority of both House and Senate.

The Vice President acts as President when the President transmits written declaration to the Speaker of the House that he is unable to discharge the powers and duties of his office.

Amendment 26.

Vote for Eighteen-Year-Olds (1971).

The right of citizens of the United States, who are 18 years of age or older, shall not be denied on account of age.

Amendment 27.

Limits on Salary Changes (1992).

No law changing the salaries of members of Congress can take effect until after the next election of Representatives.

Speech #12

Financial Guidelines

Personal Financial Guidelines Can Apply to Government

Philosophy:

- Personal finance is 80 percent behavior and 20 percent simple, time proven, common sense.
- Your biggest challenge is yourself.
- Don't try to keep up with the Jones. They're broke.
- It is painful to make changes.
- Debt is not a good financial tool to create prosperity. It creates major risk.
- Living in debt is living in bondage.
- Money is an excellent slave and a horrible master.
- Money will work for you by earning interest unless you work for money by paying interest.
- By sacrificing now you will be able to receive blessings later on.
- Acknowledge your financial weaknesses.
- Study wealth and wealthy people, and teach your children correct financial principles and practices.
- Plan and live for the future while you are living for the present.
- Envision financial freedom and build wealth to enjoy life, to invest, and to give.
- Always manage your own money.
- Maximize your investing.
- The love of money, not money, is the root of all evil.
- Avoid "Affluenza" by allowing wealth to become your God.

Scriptures:

- Romans 12:2 And be not conformed to this world: but be ye transformed by the renewing of your mind, that ye may prove what is that good, and acceptable, and perfect, will of God.
- Proverbs 22:7: The rich rules over the poor, and the borrower is servant to the lender.
- Proverbs 17:18: A man void of understanding striketh hands, and becometh surety in the presence of his friend. (It's stupid to guarantee someone else's loan.)
- Proverbs 13:22 A good man leaves an inheritance to his children's children . . ."
- Luke 14: 28 Which of you, intending to build a tower, does not sit down first and count the cost, whether he has enough to finish it . . .
- Proverbs 10:15 The rich man's wealth is his strong city. (A rich man's wealth can become his strength.)
- Proverbs 6:1 and 5 If you have signed surety, my son, . . . deliver yourself like the bird from the hand of the fowler and the gazelle from the hand of the hunter. (surety = debt)

10 Commandments (Dos)

1. Do pay a 10 percent tithing to a church or reliable charity.
2. Do develop and work a budget every month before it begins.
3. Do keep a $1,000 cash emergency fund and a 6-month emergency fund (in liquid assets).
4. Do get out of debt and stay out.
5. Do save and invest 15 percent of your gross income.
6. Do get an education: Pay as you go. Get scholarships. Look into the military to pay for it.
7. Do pay off your home by using only 15-year mortgages.
8. Do pay for things in cash, including a car.

9. Do buy appropriate insurance for auto, home, health, and long-term care, including only term life insurance.
10. Do keep your retirement, will, and estate planning current.

10 Commandments (Don'ts)

1. Do not use credit cards, debt, college loans, debt consolidation or a home equity loan as financial tools.
2. Do not use cash advance, payday loans, rent-to-own, title pawning, and tote-the-note car lots.
3. Do not lease cars or have car payments.
4. Do not purchase whole life insurance, ARMs or balloon mortgages.
5. Do not invest in gold, mobile homes, prepaid funeral expenses, or prepaid college tuition.
6. Do not lend money to or co-sign loans for friends or relatives.
7. Do not leave open debts in a divorce.
8. Do not gamble, play the lotto or try get- rich-quick formulas.
9. Do not file bankruptcy or use debt management companies.
10. Do not raise your lifestyle when you get a raise.

Speech #13

Leadership Advice

Be Private, Reflective, and Encouraging

Your objective is to resolve any disconnect with those under your direction, and promote goodwill and teamwork. Don't feel the need to preach. Give honest and hopefully useful feedback. Consider the following in general terms with specific applications:

1. Be clear and decisive. No one appreciates a weather vane. If you make a decision, stand by it. When you give direction to others and then you do have to change that decision for whatever reason, don't blame others. Just explain the reason and move on. Also, far too much time is spent trying to "cover our tracks" in order to avoid future questions or criticism. Make good decisions based upon what is best now, not what people will think.

2. Be a problem solver and not a finger pointer. Finding fault or blaming others is an easy way to look good, but it is usually a hard way to solve problems. Placing blame only partially masks the problem, and may not show reality. Observers of finger pointers will conclude that they, too, will be blamed and criticized. It encourages everyone to work below the line. (Above the line – see it, own it, solve it, and do it. Below the line or "blamestorming" – ignore/ deny, it's not my job, finger pointing, confusion, tell me what to do, and wait and see.)

3. Be a leader of growth, not a steward of stagnation. It's true that the business organization culture requires that we work within guidelines and within systems to aid employees and facilitate the work. However, it is important to remember that the employees and the work are not working to follow the guidelines or to satisfy the "system." The work is what is important, not the guidelines or system. The work will always be the same, but guidelines and systems will change. Focusing on the guidelines and systems is like looking at things upside down. It is not only demeaning to the employees, but counterproductive to the work. It's too easy to become too demanding and to draft or rely on the "letter of the law" at the expense of the "spirit of the law".

4. Be a source of faith and not a perpetuator of fear. Don't make room for fear in your organization. Be of strong faith. You have many resources. Use them wisely, and maximize their potential. Allow your leaders to see reality so they can ask questions and make decisions accordingly. When people operate in a culture of fear there is little if any effective feedback. People will say and do only what is expected or what is "politically correct." They go silent and move away if they are not already being nudged out by immature managers who don't know how to get the best out of the resources they have. Don't be afraid of feedback that is different from your own thinking or that stimulates you to progress. And, don't be afraid to give such to those who need it.

5. Manage exceptionally, not only by exception. Proper and skillful management by exception is one of many good management tools. If used in excess or on auto pilot, management by exception can be counterproductive

and cause people to either disappear off your radar or at its center to get attention. Be exceptional by working with people and focus on each individual who is doing good and not just on those who are out of line. Focusing on the exception works great in "mowing the lawn" scenarios, but is destructive when used in gardens or flowerbeds.

6. Build on strengths, not weaknesses. Everyone has weaknesses. To focus on or exploit those weaknesses demonstrates insecurity and fear. It is very difficult if not impossible for individuals to overcome their weaknesses when that is all others see or focus on. Pulling others down does not promote growth or progress. Building up and supporting will promote both growth and progress while developing good will.

7. Be grateful for others' support. Most employees are here to serve as asked and to be supportive in moving the work forward. We all have a responsibility to both do "our job" as well as help to improve business practices and policies. Be grateful for them and confident that everyone has much to contribute. The magic of managing is in maximizing on employee strengths and contributions.

Speech #14

"Not Yours to Give" –Davy Crockett

Davy Crockett and Horatio Bunce

I read the following story about Davy Crockett and sent it to all our children, asking them to read it and teach their children the principles taught therein. I recommend the same to you and your family. Please share it. My fear is that there are not enough legislators like Davy Crockett and not enough Americans like Horatio Bunce. I believe we can find such individuals and be committed to support them in elections.

Public servants should avoid lavish celebrations, personal vacationing, and public excesses. If they control themselves, the people will follow. The principles this story reveals are powerful. We must insure the limits to government if we are to preserve individual liberty.

The Story

The Not Yours to Give story was told by Colonel David Crockett, U.S. Representative from Tennessee. It was originally published in The Life of Colonel David Crockett, by Edward Sylvester Ellis. One day in the House of Representatives a bill was taken up appropriating money for the benefit of the widow of a distinguished naval officer. Several beautiful speeches had been made in its support. The Speaker was just about to put the question to a vote when Crockett arose.

"Mr. Speaker," he said, "I have as much respect for the memory of the deceased, and as much sympathy for the sufferings of the living, if suffering there be, as any man in this House, but we must not permit our respect for the dead nor our sympathy for a part of the living to lead us into an act of injustice to the balance of the living. I will not go into an argument to prove that Congress has not the power to appropriate this money as an act of charity. Every member upon this floor knows it. We have the right, as individuals, to give away as much of our own money as we please in charity; but as members of Congress we have no right so to appropriate a dollar of the public money. Some eloquent appeals have been made to us upon the ground that it is a debt due the deceased. Mr. Speaker, the deceased lived long after the close of the war; he was in office to the day of his death, and I have never heard that the government was in arrears to him.

"Every man in this House knows it is not a debt. We cannot, without the grossest corruption, appropriate this money as the payment of a debt. We have not the semblance of authority to appropriate it as charity. Mr. Speaker, I have said we have the right to give as much money of our own as we please. I am the poorest man on this floor. I cannot vote for this bill, but I will give one week's pay to the object, and if every member of Congress will do the same, it will amount to more than the bill asks."

He took his seat. Nobody replied. The bill was put upon its passage, and, instead of passing unanimously, as was generally supposed, and as, no doubt, it would, but for that speech, it received but few votes, and, of course, was lost.

Charity and Goodwill

Later, when asked by a friend why he had opposed the appropriation, Crockett gave this explanation: "Several years ago I was one evening standing on the steps of the Capitol with some other members of Congress, when our attention was attracted by a great light over in Georgetown. It was evidently a large fire. We jumped into a hack and drove over as fast as we could. In spite of all that could be done, many houses were burned and many families made houseless, and, besides, some of them had lost all but the clothes they had on. The weather was very cold, and when I saw so many women and children suffering, I felt that something ought to be done for them. The next morning, a bill was introduced appropriating $20,000 for their relief. We put aside all other business and rushed it through as soon as it could be done.

"The next summer, when it began to be time to think about election, I concluded I would take a scout around among the boys of my district. I had no opposition there, but, as the election was some time off, I did not know what might turn up. When riding one day in a part of my district in which I was more of a stranger than any other, I saw a man in a field plowing and coming toward the road. I gauged my gait so that we should meet as he came to the fence. As he came up, I spoke to the man. He replied politely, but, as I thought, rather coldly.

"I began, 'Well, friend, I am one of those unfortunate beings called candidates, and - - -

"Yes I know you. You are Colonel Crockett. I have seen you once before, and voted for you the last time you were elected. I suppose you are out electioneering now, but you had better not waste your time or mine, I shall not vote for you again."

"This was a sockdolager. I begged him to tell me what was the matter.

"Well, Colonel, it is hardly worthwhile to waste time or words upon it. I do not see how it can be mended, but you gave a vote last winter which shows that either you have not capacity to understand the Constitution, or that you are wanting in the honesty and firmness to be guided by it. In either case you are not the man to represent me. But I beg your pardon for expressing it in that way. I did not intend to avail myself of the privilege of the constituent to speak plainly to a candidate for the purpose of insulting or wounding you. I intend by it only to say that your understanding of the Constitution is very different from mine; and I will say to you what, but for my rudeness, I should not have said, that I believe you to be honest . . . But an understanding of the Constitution different from mine I cannot overlook, because the Constitution, to be worth anything, must be held sacred, and rigidly observed in all its provisions. The man who wields power and misinterprets it is the more dangerous the more honest he is.'

"I admit the truth of all you say, but there must be some mistake about it, for I do not remember that I gave any vote last winter upon any constitutional question."

"No, Colonel, there's no mistake. Though I live in the backwoods and seldom go from home, I take the papers from Washington and read very carefully all the proceedings of Congress. My papers say that last winter you voted for a bill to appropriate $20,000 to some sufferers by a fire in Georgetown. Is that true?'

'Well, my friend; I may as well own up. You have got me there. But certainly nobody will complain that a great and rich country like ours should give the insignificant sum of $20,000 to relieve its suffering women and children, particularly with a full and overflowing Treasury, and I am sure, if you had been there, you would have done just as I did."

It Is Not the Amount, It's the Principle

"It is not the amount, Colonel, that I complain of; it is the principle. In the first place, the government ought to have in the Treasury no more than enough for its legitimate purposes. But that has nothing with the question. The power of collecting and disbursing money at pleasure is the most dangerous power that can be entrusted to man, particularly under our system of collecting revenue by a tariff, which reaches every man in the country, no matter how poor he may be, and the poorer he is the more he pays in proportion to his means. What is worse, it presses upon him without his knowledge where the weight centers, for there is not a man in the United States who can ever guess how much he pays to the government. So you see, that while you are contributing to relieve one, you are drawing it from thousands who are even worse off than he. If you had the right to give anything, the amount was simply a matter of discretion with you, and you had as much right to give $20 million as $20 thousand. If you have the right to give to one, you have the right to give to all; and, as the Constitution neither defines charity nor stipulates the amount, you are at liberty to give to any and everything which you may believe, or profess to believe, is a charity, and to any amount you may think proper. You will very easily perceive what a wide door this would open for fraud and corruption and favoritism, on the one hand, and for robbing the people on the other. No, Colonel, Congress has no right to give charity. Individual members may give as much of their own money as they please, but they have no right to touch a dollar of the public money for that purpose. If twice as many houses had been burned in this county as in Georgetown, neither you nor any other member of Congress would have thought of appropriating a dollar for our relief."

"There are about two hundred and forty members of Congress. If they had shown their sympathy for the sufferers by contributing each one week's pay, it would have made over $13,000. There are plenty of wealthy men in and around Washington who could have given $20,000 without depriving themselves of even a luxury of life.

"The congressmen chose to keep their own money, which, if reports be true, some of them spend not very creditably; and the people about Washington, no doubt, applauded you for relieving them from the necessity of giving by giving what was not yours to give. The people have delegated to Congress, by the Constitution, the power to do certain things. To do these, it is authorized to collect and pay moneys, and for nothing else. Everything beyond this is usurpation, and a violation of the Constitution.

"So you see, Colonel, you have violated the Constitution in what I consider a vital point. It is a precedent fraught with danger to the country, for when Congress once begins to stretch its power beyond the limits of the Constitution, there is no limit to it, and no security for the people. I have no doubt you acted honestly, but that does not make it any better, except as far as you are personally concerned, and you see that I cannot vote for you."

A Lesson Learned

"I tell you I felt streaked. I saw if I should have opposition, and this man should go to talking, he would set others to talking, and in that district I was a gone fawn-skin. I could not answer him, and the fact is, I was so fully convinced that he was right, I did not want to. But I must satisfy him, and I said to him: "Well, my friend, you hit the nail upon the head when you said I had not sense enough to understand the Constitution. I intended to be guided by it, and thought I had studied it fully. I have heard many speeches in Congress about the powers of Congress, but what you have said here at your plow has got more hard, sound sense in it than all the fine speeches I ever heard. If I had ever taken the view of it that you have, I would have put my head into the fire before I would have given that vote; and if you will forgive me and vote for me again, if I ever vote for another unconstitutional law I wish I may be shot."

"He laughingly replied; 'Yes, Colonel, you have sworn to that once before, but I will trust you again upon one condition. You say that you are convinced that your vote was wrong. Your acknowledgment of it will do more good than beating you for it. If, as you go around the district, you will tell people about this vote, and that you are satisfied it was wrong, I will not only vote for you, but will do what I can to keep down opposition, and, perhaps, I may exert some little influence in that way."

"If I don't," said I, "I wish I may be shot; and to convince you that I am in earnest in what I say I will come back this way in a week or ten days, and if you will get up a gathering of the people, I will make a speech to them. Get up a barbecue, and I will pay for it."

Horatio Bunce

"No, Colonel, we are not rich people in this section, but we have plenty of provisions to contribute for a barbecue, and some to spare for those who have none. The push of crops will be over in a few days, and we can then afford a day for a barbecue. This is Thursday; I will see to getting it up on Saturday week. Come to my house, and we will go together, and I promise you a very respectable crowd to see and hear you."

"Well, I will be here. But one thing more before I say good-bye. I must know your name."

"My name is Bunce."

"Not Horatio Bunce?"

"Yes."

"Well, Mr. Bunce, I never saw you before, though you say you have seen me, but I know you very well. I am glad I have met you, and very proud that I may hope to have you for my friend."

"It was one of the luckiest hits of my life that I met him. He mingled but little with the public, but was widely known for his remarkable intelligence and incorruptible integrity, and for a heart brimful and running over with kindness and benevolence, which showed themselves not only in words but in acts. He was the oracle of the whole country around him, and his fame had extended far beyond the circle of his immediate acquaintance. Though I had never met him before, I had heard much of him, and but for this meeting it is very likely I should have had opposition, and had been beaten. One thing is very certain, no man could now stand up in that district under such a vote.

"At the appointed time I was at his house, having told our conversation to every crowd I had met, and to every man I stayed all night with, and I found that it gave the people an interest and a confidence in me stronger than I had ever seen manifested before.

"Though I was considerably fatigued when I reached his house, and, under ordinary circumstances, should have gone early to bed, I kept him up until midnight, talking about the principles and affairs of government, and got more real, true knowledge of them than I had got all my life before.

"I have known and seen much of him since, for I respect him—no, that is not the word—I reverence and love him more than any living man, and I go to see him two or three times every year; and I will tell you, sir, if everyone who professes to be a Christian lived and acted and enjoyed it as he does, the religion of Christ would take the world by storm.

"But to return to my story. The next morning we went to the barbecue, and, to my surprise, found about a thousand men there. I met a good many whom I had not known before, and they and my friend introduced me around until I had got pretty well acquainted. At least, they all knew me.

"In due time notice was given that I would speak to them. They gathered up around a stand that had been erected. I opened my speech by saying: 'Fellow-citizens, I present myself before you today feeling like a new man. My eyes have lately been opened to truths which ignorance or prejudice, or both, had heretofore hidden from my view. I feel that I can today offer you the ability to render you more valuable service than I have ever been able to render before. I am here today more for the purpose of acknowledging my error than to seek your votes. That I should make this acknowledgment is due to myself as well as to you. Whether you will vote for me is a matter for your consideration only.'

"I went on to tell them about the fire and my vote for the appropriation and then told them why I was satisfied it was wrong. I closed by saying: 'And now, fellow-citizens, it remains only for me to tell you that the most of the speech you have listened to with so much interest was simply a repetition of the arguments by which your neighbor, Mr. Bunce, convinced me of my error.' It is the best speech I ever made in my life, but he is entitled to the credit for it. And now I hope he is satisfied with his convert and that he will get up here and tell you so.

"He came upon the stand and said: 'Fellow-citizens, It affords me great pleasure to comply with the request of Colonel Crockett. I have always considered him a thoroughly honest man, and I am satisfied that he will faithfully perform all that he has promised you today.' He went down, and there went up from that crowd such a shout for Davy Crockett as his name never called forth before.

"I am not much given to tears, but I was taken with a choking then and felt some big drops rolling down my cheeks. And I tell you now that the remembrance of those few words spoken by such a man, and the honest, hearty shout they produced, is worth more to me than all the honors I have received and all the reputation I have ever made, or ever shall make, as a member of Congress.

No Charity in Government

"Now, Sir," concluded Crockett, "You know why I made that speech yesterday. There is one thing now to which I will call your attention. You remember that I proposed to give a week's pay. There are in that House many very wealthy men who think nothing of spending a week's pay, or a dozen of them, for a dinner or a wine party when they have something to accomplish by it.

"Some of those same men made beautiful speeches upon the great debt of gratitude which the country owed the deceased—a debt which could not be paid by money—and the insignificance and worthlessness of money, particularly so insignificant a sum as $10,000, when weighed against the honor of the nation. Yet not one of them responded to my proposition. Money with them is nothing but trash when it is to come out of the people. But it is the one great thing for which most of them are striving for. And many of them sacrifice honor, integrity, and justice to obtain it."

Moral of the Story

The federal government has no Constitutional right to take from one citizen and give to another.

Speech #15

Civil War – Gettysburg

Appomattox Court House, Virginia

In early April, 1865, Confederate General Robert E. Lee and the tattered remnants of his Army of Northern Virginia camped in Petersburg, not far from Richmond, the Confederate capital in eastern Virginia. They were running out of soldiers and supplies. Ulysses S. Grant's Union soldiers waited outside the city for nine months. When Lee finally took his starving army out to find food, the Union forces entered Petersburg and Richmond. Lee found his path blocked. Finally defeated, General Lee had no choice but to surrender.

Within a week, on April 9, Grant and Lee met in the town of Appomattox Court House in southern Virginia. After four years, the Civil War was finally over. Over 600,000 men had died, and over a million more had been wounded. The South lay in ruins. Hatred between the two sides ran incredibly strong and deep.

At the place of surrender, the defeated Confederate Army came face-to-face with their despised victors as they marched past Union solders to stack their arms. General Grant gave Major General Joshua Lawrence Chamberlain from Maine the great honor of accepting the surrender.

Picture it with me, if you will: Saber in hand, Chamberlain sits ramrod straight astride his horse on the far right of the Union Regiments lining both sides of the street. Confederate Major General John Brown Gordon and the first of the Confederate brigades approaches from the right. As Gordon comes abreast his position, Chamberlain does something totally unexpected and without precedent. This how he described it:

"The momentous meaning of this occasion impressed me deeply. I resolved to mark it by some token of recognition, which could be no other than a salute of arms. Well aware of the responsibility assumed, and of the criticisms that would follow . . . I sought no authority nor asked forgiveness. Before us in proud humiliation stood the embodiment of manhood: men whom neither toils and sufferings, nor the fact of death, nor disaster, nor hopelessness could bend from their resolve; standing before us now, thin, worn, and famished, but erect, and with eyes looking level into ours, waking memories that bound us together as no other bond. Is not such manhood to be welcomed back into a Union so tested and assured?

Instructions had been given; and when the head of each division column comes opposite our group, our bugle sounds the signal and instantly our whole line from right to left, regiment by regiment in succession, gives the soldier's salutation, from the "order arms" to the old "carry" – the marching salute. Gordon at the head of the column, riding with heavy spirit and downcast face, catches the sound of shifting arms, looks up, and, taking the meaning, wheels superbly, making with himself and his horse one uplifted figure, with profound salutation as he drops the point of his sword to the boot toe; then facing to his own command, gives word for his successive brigades to pass us with the same position of the manual—honor answering honor. On our part not a sound of trumpet more, nor roll of drum; not a cheer, nor word nor whisper of vain-glorying, nor motion of man standing again at the order, but an awed stillness rather, and breath-holding, as if it were the passing of the dead!"

That noble gesture by an honorable man began the healing of a nation. So, you might ask, out of all the Union generals, why did Grant choose Chamberlain?

Gettysburg, Pennsylvania

Let's back up a couple of years. In 1863, the war wasn't going well for the North. Lee's Confederate Army had won just about every battle and were feeling very confident. And now, in late June, they had marched up the Shenandoah Valley into Pennsylvania, with Washington, D.C., as their objective. It was a desperate time for President Abraham Lincoln and the United States.

If the seemingly invincible Lee made it to Washington, the war might be over and the Union severed forever. In late June, Lincoln ordered Union troops under General George Mead to intercept Lee's army. On the 1st of July these two mighty armies (97,000 troops on the Union side and nearly 80,000 on the Confederate) came together where multiple roads meet in a small town called Gettysburg in south-central Pennsylvania, 90 miles north and a little west of Washington, D.C.

Union and Confederate Positions

Heavy fighting ensued on the first day as the armies of both sides maneuvered for position. That evening, the Union troops took up a position on some high ground south of the town. The Confederates took positions to the west and north.

As the sun set and the musket fire and the cries of battle slowly died out, Union forces began to dig into the rocky soil, knowing they would need all the protection they could muster on the following day.

That night, at the White House, President Abraham Lincoln recounted this:

". . . oppressed by the gravity of our affairs, I went to my room . . . and locked the door and got down on my knees before almighty God and prayed to Him mightily for victory at Gettysburg. I told Him that this war was His, and our cause His cause, but we could not stand another Fredricksburg or Chancellorsville. Then and there I made a solemn vow to almighty God that if He would stand by our boys at Gettysburg, I would stand by Him. And after that, I don't know how it was, and I cannot explain it, soon a sweet comfort crept into my soul. The feeling came that God had taken the whole business into His own hands, and that things would go right at Gettysburg."

The next day, the Union soldiers waited through the hot day for the Confederates to make their move. About 3:00 the attack finally began. Picture it if you can . . .

Battlefield from Center of Union Lines

Now the fog of war often results in critical mistakes, and this battle was no different. Well after the Confederate attack had started, a potentially fatal error was discovered by a Union soldier. Their left flank had been left totally uncovered. Were the Confederates to get behind the Union lines, things would go very wrong at Gettysburg. The battle, and most likely, the war would be lost.

Realizing their grave mistake, Union generals quickly ordered the 20th Maine Volunteers, led by then- Colonel Joshua Chamberlain, to take a position on a steep hill called Little Round Top at the very south of the line. They were told to hold the position at all costs. The men of the 20th scampered up the backside of the hill and almost immediately began taking fire from the attacking Confederates, who had also discovered the unmanned flank.

Little Round Top

Now the 35-year-old Chamberlain had only been a colonel for a month and was newly appointed to the command. He was a soft-spoken college professor, a scholar, not a professional soldier. He spoke seven languages fluently and was a very religious man, having seriously considered the ministry before electing academia as his life's pursuit. But now he found himself in one of the greatest battles in history, defending the most critical point on the battlefield with too few men.

He quickly strung his men out along the ridge, doubling the normal space between men, to cover the line. He angled half of them back to the east to try and cover the southern flank better. The terrible battle raged, with thousands being cut down on both sides of the line.

Around 7:30 p.m., several regiments of Confederate troops from Alabama converged on the 20th Maine's position to try to break the flank. The Alabamans attacked again and again, each time being repulsed by Chamberlain's men. But it couldn't last. Many of the 20th had been killed, scores were wounded, including Chamberlain himself, and they were nearly out of ammunition.

As the Rebels surged up the hill once again, Chamberlain astonished even his own troops by giving an order contrary to all logic and military doctrine. He yelled to his men to fix their bayonets, leave their defensive positions on the high ground and charge the enemy. He ordered the far left flank to make a sweeping wheel turn, like a closing gate, and they all charged down the steep hill at the Confederates coming up.

The move so surprised the Alabamans that most surrendered, and the rest turned and ran. The flank was secured, the battle ultimately won, and Lee's path to Washington forever blocked. The Confederate Army never encroached in the North again.

Single Most Significant Incident of the War

The battle for Little Round Top and Chamberlain's decisive order was the single most significant incident of the war. I also believe that it was not by accident that a man like Joshua Lawrence Chamberlain was where he was at that critical moment. Abraham Lincoln's fervent prayer of the night before was answered by an honorable man. Lincoln was more concerned about being on God's side than God being on his side.

Was the quiet college professor a hero? Indeed he was. During the war, he was wounded six times and had six horses shot out from under him, but each time he returned to lead his men.

So, did Joshua Lawrence Chamberlain know he was being divinely guided that day on Little Round Top? The title of his autobiography is instructive. It's called, In the Hands of Providence. He knew he was an instrument of God in keeping the country together.

Speech #16

Solving Big Problems

We can solve big problems with simple solutions. Perhaps you have heard the story of the truck that got stuck under the overpass because it was just one inch too tall. The driver couldn't move forward or backward. The fire department could not solve the problem. Engineers were brought in as experts to consult and give advice in order to get the truck out of the way, so traffic could pass through again. They finally concluded that the only solution was to cut the top of the truck off. A small boy stepped forward and said, "Hey Mister. Why don't you just let some air out of the tires so the truck will be short enough to go through under the bridge?" The experts had never thought of that simple solution. Within minutes, the problem was solved.

Corral Dig-Out

My problem-solving story is about digging out of a problem. I'll call it the "Corral Dig-Out Story." When I was a young man growing up in Idaho, my employer was the Carlson family who lived in Groveland, just outside of Blackfoot, Idaho. They operated a family dairy and raised crops. I was 15 years old, six-foot tall, and could work all day as long as they fed me. During the summers, I hauled hay, built fences and dug ditches. Digging ditches is another whole story. In the fall, I bucked sacks of potatoes and emptied them in the spud cellar.

Well, my corral dig-out story began early one spring after a particularly harsh winter. Temperatures quickly rose, and everything thawed out and pastures were turning green. Mr.

Carlson seemed almost embarrassed as he pointed to the corral gate that opened inward. He explained that during a blizzard that winter, he had not let the cows out to the pasture for almost a week. He had just fed the herd in the corral and spread straw to keep them clean. The manure level got up higher than the gate and froze solid, so he couldn't open the gates.

Now, everything was thawed out and the cows were wading in a two-foot deep pool of green soupy manure. Carlson was running out of feed and needed to get the herd out of the corral and into the pasture. He humbly shook his head in apology and said, with his hand shielding his lips from the twins running up to say hello, "Dale, as you can see, we are in deep (he spelled) D.U.N.G. We really need your help." He then gave me a pair of hip wading boots, a manure fork, scoop shovel and a clean pair of rubber gloves.

I put on the boots and gloves and climbed over the fence, waded in knee deep and began working. The odor was strong, and occasionally I dug up a pocket of ammonia fumes that burned my nose and made my eyes water. At times, I thought I wasn't making any progress. It took a long time and it was hard work, but I got the job done.

Now, our nation has some serious problems that we need to work on. I love the United States of America, and it loves me. We may not be in over our heads yet, but we are in knee deep and need to get to work to dig our way out of our problems.

Speech #17

Our Dreams, Our Wars

Pilgrims Dream

The first Pilgrims came to the New World to start a new life and worship as they wanted. There followed a long and challenging time of New World colonization by European countries. The promise of opportunities brought more and more people to North America.

American Revolution

Many years after the Pilgrims, the dream of self-government was finally realized when our Founding Fathers established a new nation, with a strong Constitution. During these days and the following decades, there was rapid expansion, excessive greed, unjust cruelty and blatant hypocrisy among many people in all parts of the nation.

Civil War

Such dynamic expansion resulted in growing pride, uncontrolled greed and contention on almost everyone's part. The nation became divided, father against son and friend against friend. This great split was over both ideology and economic interests. The Southern States seceded, and a great Civil War began. President Lincoln was forced to exert wartime powers in order to win the war and preserve the Union. Victory by the North finally solved the lingering problem of slavery. But, it did not solve the problem of tremendous prejudice and inequality.

During the Reconstruction period after the war, the Federal government became very strong. Each President after the war got used to exerting a little more power than the last. Radical political and economic philosophies such as socialism and communism were being tried around the world. Some of these found their way into the minds of Americans.

1900s

In early 1912, Arizona and New Mexico were added to the Union as the forty-seventh and forty-eighth states. The following year, in 1913, a series of unexpected events and mood swings in public opinion occurred. The House, the Senate, and the Presidency were all controlled by one party. The feeling of optimism and socialism was sweeping the country. This was coupled with the ambitions of many for expanding the power of the federal government and in building up the U.S. military.

The 16th Amendment, introducing a personal income tax, took over three years to be ratified, but the 17th Amendment, allowing Senators to be elected by popular vote instead of by state legislatures, took less than eleven months. By April of 1913, the votes of Congress, the President, and all but a few dissenting states dramatically changed the course of the United States.

Over time, there have been amendments that protect citizens, but others—the 16th Amendment regarding personal income tax, and the 17th Amendment regarding direct election of Senators—empower the federal government. No amount of debate, political gymnastics, or grassroots effort will ever amount to anything until these two amendments have been repealed. Until that happens, the Federal government can tax U.S. citizens without limitation, and the state governments will have no power to keep Senators accountable.

Continuous War, Economic Turmoil, and Moral Decay

Since 1900, there has been continuous military intervention, war and conflict. There are increased attempts to control and monitor economic booms and busts. There has been a gradual introduction and acceptance of government entitlement programs with a dramatic rise in substance addiction, immorality and family disintegration.

Our Wars

We are at war, but not for territory. We are fighting for the high ground. We are in the midst of a great contest of ideas, principles and emotions. This struggle is escalating into dangerous conflict and potential civil unrest. The thundering shot has been fired and has been heard around the world.

We are not asked to cross the freezing Delaware River to re-capture Trenton, New Jersey, as George Washington did, but we must pass through ridicule to again secure religious freedom for all to worship how, where, or what they may.

We are not charged to keep the high ground at Gettysburg, but we must keep the high ground of personal morality. We have not been ordered to sweep down from Little Round Top with bayonets on empty muskets, but we must repulse the onslaught of pornography and remove its protection behind freedom of speech.

We cannot afford to be bogged down any longer in the dark trench warfare of indebtedness. We must be on the offensive and fight diligently to eliminate the national debt. We are not asked to storm the beaches of Normandy, but we must steadily move forward in unity with a united voice of equality, opportunity and prosperity.

Strengthen and Rebuild Within

We are not asked to provide the resources for the reconstruction of Europe or Japan after World War II, but we must consider the renovation of our transportation and communication systems in the United States.

We are not asked to forge a new path, but to return to the original path of the Founding Fathers. Let us join in one voice and in one effort to try this new experiment. Focus on solutions rather than people or problems. Resolve, not just revolve. Incentivize people to produce, save, and plan for the future.

Provide for the Common Defense

Diminish foreign aid and international intervention. Strengthen military defenses at home. Take care of our veterans. Distance ourselves from United Nations involvement and allow another country to be their host.

Best Practices and Sound Principles

We must use zero-based budgeting and spend only what's in the treasury. We must make museums, parks, and public services self-funding. Each state and community shares the costs with users of airports, terminals, highways, tunnels and bridges, etc.

Instead of an income tax, a transition 10 percent flat tax could be used for a time. After that, the federal government would be funded by the states. We can eliminate all savings, death and inheritance taxes.

We must use Social Security and Medicaid money only for those purposes. We must bring manufacturing back to the United States. We need to establish a Composite Commodity Standard to back the U.S. dollar. We need to audit and/or replace the Federal Reserve. We must review and eliminate all treaties not in our best interest. We must become energy independent.

Legitimate Legislation and Voting Reform

In Congress, demand concise and understandable legislation to be read before being voted on. Veto any legislation that does not meet these requirements.

End illegal immigration and reinstate English as our national language. Require voter ID and registration, along with the ability to read, write and speak English, for all voters. Require manual verification of vote counts for national elections.

The American Dream

The American Dream is to be a free, independent and prosperous nation of good people.

We are a nation of all races and religions.

We are a nation of immigrants, risk takers and good neighbors.

We are a nation that values economic and military strength as well as environmental awareness.

Being an American means so many things to so many people, but in the end, it is all based on our Constitution, the rule of law, and a government of, by, and for the people.

Speech #18

Blackfoot Announcement

Introduction

Thank you for allowing me to speak to you today. Some of you are old friends or children of friends. Some may not know who I am or what I'm doing here. I'm excited to tell you.

Before I do, I'd like to tell you that wherever I have lived around the world, Blackfoot is still my home town. When telling people where I'm from, many people know someone from Blackfoot. They had a roommate. They knew a missionary. They are or were related to someone, or they had been through Blackfoot on their way to Utah, Montana, or Canada.

At Boston College, I was the only student from Idaho. I'd tell my teammates and friends about the famous Idaho potatoes. One night after a late basketball practice, we came into a deserted cafeteria. We were served our food. As I moved my tray along the line to where there was a new French fry machine, I saw the oval metal label stamped with "American Potato, Blackfoot Idaho, Potato Capital of the World."

I shouted out, "Hey guys, you've got to see this!" I was much more credible after that. Blackfoot is a very special place. It's good to be from here, and it's good to be home.

Announcement

It is with great honor, excitement, and humility that I come before you today to announce that I am officially running as a candidate for President of the United States of America. I've been a long time in preparation. This decision has not been an easy one to make.

However, with good fortune and the grace of God, I will be successful. I ask for your prayers and for your support. I ask that you read the materials on my website to get better acquainted with me and with my message. I also ask you to share this message with your family and friends.

I invite you to kindle the fire of liberty in your heart and the hearts of your children and those around you. Read the Constitution, and pray for God's Holy Spirit to lift you up so you, too, can do your part in this important time in the history of our nation. I promise you that, if you do this, you will have a new awakening of truth and liberty. It will flow into your mind and heart.

I know that not all of you will agree with my message. None of you will probably agree with everything I represent and say. But, I hope you will consider my message and support me on those things we do have in common.

Who I Am

Now, I'd like to step back in time and reminisce a little about this special place in the Snake River Valley. I was born in a house in Shelley. When I was a year old, my family moved to Blackfoot. It was here that I discovered who I was and that I had a work to do. It was here that I was nurtured by my family and helped by my friends. I was tutored by great leaders, school teachers and coaches.

We lived down on 285 South University Street. It was there when I was a little boy that my mother told me that one day

I could someday be President of the United States. In that humble house, I was inspired to do many things.

We attended Church in a chapel that has long since been taken down and replaced. My first memory of church was when my sister Dian took me by the hand as we walked up the front stairs. I bent over and picked up a pink blob of chewing gum. It still had some sweet flavor in it, and some sand. She cried because she couldn't get it out of my mouth.

Another day, my teacher cried because she couldn't get me to climb back down the pipes that went from the floor up to the ceiling.

It was here in Blackfoot that I found my first friends and heroes. I met my dear friends in a fist fight. After punching each other out, we shook hands and have been friends ever since. It was Barrett Packer who was my idol. He was a great student and athlete and I wanted to be just like him. I watched everything he did. He became a dentist and practiced in Farmington, Utah. I still admire him.

In the corner classroom of the Blackfoot Junior High School, I took Algebra from my father. I behaved myself and made sure my homework was always done.

Many people inspired me to set goals and believe that I could do anything that I decided to do. I remember people always asking me what I wanted to be when I grew up. I would answer, "A doctor." "What kind of a doctor?" they would ask. "A good one!" Now that I'm older, I still want to help, serve and heal people, but in a different way. You may be wondering what kind of a president I will be. I want to be a good one!

By today's standards, we lived below the poverty level. My bedroom was the back porch. It wasn't heated. It was freezing cold in the winter. Snowdrifts formed under the door and my drink of water was frozen in the morning. When I woke up, I quickly ran into the warm kitchen to enjoy a hot breakfast with my father. In the summers, mosquitos came in through the broken screens and the ventilation was very poor. In comparison to my friends in town, we were poor, but we got by.

Some of my first friends were Native Americans. Arty Hevawah, Larry Johnson, Andy Teton and Abraham Watson were great athletes. I remember visiting them on the Fort Hall Indian Reservation during the summers with my father. While he did his business with the parents, I played and swam and remember not wanting to go home. When I saw their homes, I felt like we were rich. Wealth is relative. There will always be others who have more and who have less.

My fifth-grade teacher, Mrs. Hall, said I was a born leader. I believed her. Several of my teachers told me that. I thought that it was bad to be a leader because they told me that when I got into trouble. I later learned that they were trying to inspire me to be my best.

Somehow, I found myself in quite a few fist fights. I was big for my age and some of the older boys wanted to put me in my place. They were bullies, but I stood up to each one of them. One night when we were leaving the swimming pool, one boy insisted on fighting again. He had beaten me up before, but I'd had enough. After he had pushed and slapped me several times, I put my towel and swimming suit down and punched him as hard as I could right in the nose. He got up and I did the same thing two more times. When he realized that I was not going to take it anymore, he apologized and we shook hands.

He never bothered me after that. It was then that I learned that you must be strong and defend yourself.

When I was sixteen, I felt like I was a man and could do manly things. One summer, we were working on replacing the roof on our house. I clearly remember my father's reaction and answer when I asked him when the right time to kiss a girl was. Without delay or looking up from hammering nails, he said, "Dale, if you're going to kiss a girl, you want to first make sure she has clean spit!" My brother and I started laughing so hard. I almost fell off the roof.

Blackfoot Was Where I Became Who I am

I learned how to work here in Blackfoot, where I sold papers on the streets and in every bar in town. I hauled sprinkler pipes and harvested potatoes, beets and hay in Rose, Groveland, Riverside, Fort Hall and Pingree.

As a boy and young man living in Blackfoot, I felt like it was my responsibility to make the world a better place. I knew that I had a job to do and I needed to prepare myself. Abraham Lincoln once said, "I will prepare myself and my time will come." I feel like I have prepared myself and that my time has come.

I always felt greatness inside of me and wanted to be discovered. There were brief moments of heroism in sports. For me, Blackfoot was the center of the universe, and I thought that high school sports were the center of Blackfoot. I loved basketball, football and baseball. When I was a junior, I threw a football 96 yards. On another day, I think I threw it 100 yards, but there was no one there to measure it for me.

My true love, however, was basketball. I wanted to be just like Bob Cousey. He was the Michael Jordan or James LeBron of my day. I'm so thankful for my teachers like Mr. Clark and my coach like Art Gardner who tried to guide me.

I will always be grateful to Frank Fulmer for helping me get a scholarship to play football at BYU. After my mission, I played basketball at Dixie Junior College and then transferred to Boston College in Massachusetts, where I met Mary-Jo, who became my wife.

What I Want to Do

Can any good come out of Blackfoot? Yes, a lot of great people have come from here, and I hope to be one of them. I want to do my part.

What I want to accomplish in this campaign, along with winning the office of President, is to inspire all citizens to read and become more familiar with the Constitution of the United States of America. I hope to inspire many people to become more involved in the political process. Not just to vote, but also to campaign for important issues and causes. I hope many of you will become candidates and run for office and be good agents for important changes. Thank you for your support.

Speech #19

Chinese Way

Introduction

Da Jaihao! My name is Dale Christensen, and I am a candidate to be the President of the United States. I know you don't know me, but I hope you will get to know me better.

China is a beautiful country, and the Chinese people are a beautiful people. Both China and the United States have long and interesting histories covering thousands of years. Unfortunately, people in the United States don't know much about Chinese history, nor do the Chinese know much about the ancient history of the Americas. Hopefully, one day we will become closer friends and know each other better.

Early Memories

My first recollection of China was as a young boy in the early 1950s and 1960s, praying each day before our family meals for the children in China who had no food to eat. Perhaps some of you were those children I was praying for. Ever since then I have wanted to help China have what I have.

As a child, I was shown pictures of Chinese children and told they were not allowed to pray to God. I was told that a "Bamboo Curtain" was constructed around the borders of China so no one could go in or get out. So, I also prayed that one day I would be able to come to China and help feed the children and teach them to pray.

Aunt Bertha

Shortly after being married, while studying law and working on Capitol Hill in Washington, D.C., in 1976, my wife and I lived with Aunt Bertha, who had come from Hangchow, now Hangzhou, in the early 1920s. She raised her family there until they were asked to leave in 1950. She would tell us many stories about her experiences and love for the Chinese people, Chinese history and Chinese food. We prayed that someday we would be able to come to China.

MBA Program

In 1998, our prayers were answered. I began working for a company that allowed me to visit China many times. Then I taught in the MBA program at USTC in Hefei, Anhui. Everyone was so kind to my wife and me, and we loved our two years there in 2000 and 2001. We made many friends.

Chinese Way

When I first came to USTC, I heard about some of the famous sayings of Dung Xiao Ping regarding opening up to the West. For example, "When you open the window to let the light in, some flies will come in also." I warned my MBA students to only let the good things in from the West. If you don't, you will begin to have some of the same problems we have in the U.S.A. I told them, "Take in the best and leave the rest."

While in China, I was a little sad to see so many sweet foods and candy begin sold in stores. I was sad to see pornography visible on the streets of China. I do not say this to criticize in any way, because we have our own problems in the United States. I want only the best for both of our countries.

I see China progressing in the world. I was once told by a Chinese student that China wanted to increase personal freedoms and to have more democracy. But, China does not want these things the U.S. way, but the Chinese way. I believe each country should have its own sovereignty, government, customs and laws. Others should respect these so we can better work with one another.

Freedom and Democracy

When I asked my MBA students what was China's greatest challenge, they would respond, "Too many people." When I asked what China's great asset was, they said, "We have a huge market!" Your greatest challenge is also your greatest asset. I'm sure you will meet these great challenges because you have great people.

Prepare and Forgive

With your permission, I will share with you two personal recommendations. I do not share these by way of criticism, but only by way of suggestion. The first is to be prepared. The second is to forgive.

Preparation is important for all people of all nations. We live in turbulent times, and I feel it is my duty to warn my neighbor. You are my neighbor and my friend. It would be wise if every Chinese home had a supply of rice, dried beans, and other basic food supplies. When personal challenges arise or when natural disasters occur, you can better provide for our own family as well as help others in need.

Forgiveness is a wonderful medicine for our minds and hearts. If we forgive, we can also be forgiving. This brings peace and happiness to everyone. I understand the terrible things that occurred during World War II and the deep feelings that still exist. It is my prayer that someday all the Chinese people and the Chinese government can forgive those who did these terrible things. As we all leave the horrors of the past behind, we are free to look to the future with hope.

The Best Way

A United States president, Ronald Reagan, wrote,

"A grade school class in Somerville, Massachusetts, recently wrote to me to say, 'We studied about countries and found out that each country in our world is beautiful and that we need each other. People look a little different from each other, but we're still people who need the same things. We want peace. We want to be able to get along with one another. We want freedom and justice. We want to be friends. We want no wars. We want to be able to talk to one another. We want to be able to travel around the world without fear.'"

I believe we can find the best way to work together. It may not be the American way or the Chinese way, but it may be the better or best way. Let us be friends. Let us appreciate our differences and work together to make the world a better place.

Speech #20

To China:
A New City for the United Nations Headquarters

Introduction

Da Jiahao. My name is Dale Christensen, and I am a professor at the University of Science and Technology of China located in Hefei City. I am a visiting professor, teaching in the business school and MBA program. My wife and I both love China with its delicious food, rich culture, and history, but most of all, we love the Chinese people.

I give my greetings and best wishes to everyone. I want to plant in you the seed of an idea that will capture the hearts and minds of every Chinese person as well as the people of all nations of the earth. It is an idea whose time has come and whose place is here in China!

Value of an Idea

First, let me ask you. What is the value of a simple idea? Over the many centuries past, can we begin to measure the power or the expanse of ideas that have moved individuals and nations toward their destinies? It is said that an idea may be more powerful than the strongest army or economic and political force. Such powerful ideas create this strength and guide these forces.

The world is hungry for such ideas. The idea I am about to share with you will satisfy the largest of appetites; with the promise that China, Anhui Province, Hefei City, and the whole world will benefit by its acceptance and implementation. This idea embraces and supports all of China's economic development efforts, including APEC, entering the WTO, and winning the 2008 Olympic games.

In preface to describing this idea, I would like to emphasize the dream of China becoming one of the world's greatest leading nations. The question is not if, but when? In order for China to become such, China must be a true leader—leading the way in creativity and innovation—a leader with integrity and a leader with vision.

Future of the United Nations

This idea's business development plan can initially be written and facilitated by the MBA students at USTC working together with students from all over the globe. This plan is now called UN Vision 2020. This name refers to both the year 2020 and to the term used for "perfect vision or perfect eyesight." It describes the development of the "new home" for the United Nations to be located near Hefei City. I've been told that one translation for the name Hefei means "where two rivers come together." What better place is there than here, for all nations to come together.

The Olympics 2008 games will soon be hosted in Beijing. Tourism will increase dramatically and people from all over the world will come and discover and continue to develop the tremendous opportunities and advantages of doing business here. It is an opportune time for China to extend the invitation for the United Nations to come here and enjoy its long history, rich culture and abundant potential that China has to offer.

United Nations City

By the year 2020, the United Nations City will be the best planned and most modern city on the planet. Let your imagination see a magnificent city surrounded by a Great Wall and landscaped with beautiful parks and golf courses, lakes and waterways. This city will include the following:

- An international airport, with flights from all major cities around the world.
- United Nations buildings, to be its home for the next 50 to 100 years.
- Various country's consulate offices, housing, office and retail buildings, hotels and restaurants, theaters, churches and museums with each country's unique architecture, decoration and atmosphere.
- A UN University with the best international business and law schools, medical hospital and research center, language institutes and sports stadiums and facilities to host future Olympic games and all kinds of sports including western rodeos, American baseball, ice skating and ice hockey etc.
- As the world's largest tourist destination some of the supreme attractions will include the greatest known Disney World, Water World and Zoos etc. yet to be built and enjoyed.
- The UN Music & Arts Center will be the next "Hollywood frontier" of music, art, film, entertainment and culture.
- Adventure and exercise centers for rock climbing, swimming and weight lifting along with lots of water sports and leisure on the connecting waterways and Lake Chao.

World in One City

Visitors will be able to "tour the world in one city." The city's infrastructure will include:

Futuristic elevated rail transportation systems with speed trains and super-highways coming from many major cities. Traffic will be facilitated and controlled as no other city has been able to do before.

There will be canals, elevators, people movers, walkways, roadways with bike and running trails connecting everything from buildings, airport and sports centers, etc.

This one-of-a-kind city will have traditional, modern, and futuristic architecture and engineering designs of covered and connecting buildings using the best of construction materials with advanced heating, air conditioning and sound systems.

This city will be the most unique and enviable city in the world. Truly, it will be "the best of the best" and the "most desirable city" in which to live. It will attract an unlimited abundance of economic and technological development. This unique city will join with Beijing, Shanghai, Shenzen and Hong Kong as another pillar of power and stability for China and the world.

May this idea be planted in your fertile soil and may it take root as you nourish it. And eventually, may it blossom and bear the fruit of unity, peace and prosperity.

Speech #21

To Women

"The world has enough women who are tough; we need women who are tender. There are enough women who are coarse; we need women who are kind. There are enough women who are rude; we need women who are refined. We have enough women of fame and fortune; we need more women of faith. We have enough greed; we need more goodness. We have enough vanity; we need more virtue. We have enough popularity; we need more purity."

- Margaret Nadauld

Equal but Different

Men and women are equal in every way before the supreme law of the land. There is no question that many women are more intelligent and more capable than many men. They can excel, compete and perform as well as men in almost every imaginable area and sphere of influence. In some ways, men are not able nor were they ever meant to excel, compete with or perform better than women. However, before God and before each other, men and women are different.

Regardless of these differences, women deserve the same respect, recognition and reward for work they do. If a woman does the same work that a man does, she should receive the same pay. While everyone may not be satisfied with where they are or where they want society to be, there has been enormous progress. Every individual should have the right to choose their own destiny and not be criticized nor discriminated against.

I am sympathetic regarding women's issues and congratulate women in general for their tremendous contributions and influence. Another whole speech can be dedicated to the achievements of women in the arts and sciences and the many contributions to mankind in all areas. Another speech should focus on protecting women from degradation through pornography, sex trafficking and abortion. However, in this speech, I want to focus on the feminine qualities of women and encourage all women not to diminish their greatest natural strengths in those qualities that make them different from men.

I am a man and have been tremendously influenced by great women in my life. I acknowledge our equality and our differences and address the following, not to diminish our equality, but to acknowledge our differences and to encourage all women not to forfeit their divine nature in pursuit of temporal goals. So in that spirit, I will direct my remarks.

Influence in the World

Women have a special intuition to do good and to be good. From age immemorial, societies have relied on the moral force of women. The moral foundation provided by women is one of the most beneficial influences to the common good.

Women need to protect and cultivate their moral force and influence. Preserve the innate virtue and unique gifts you bring with you into this world. Dress modestly. Speak kindly. Conduct yourself with purity. You cannot lift others if you are not virtuous.

Women are adept at instilling such qualities as faith, courage, empathy, and refinement. They work for good in all their relationships, from their families to their countries, and beyond out in the world.

Unselfishly, women sacrifice a number of pleasures and possessions for higher priorities. The demands on women are many, and tasks often repetitive and mundane. Their contributions are often underappreciated. The world should be grateful for the influence of good women.

Role in Creation

The most sacred role of women is in the creation of life. Women should be guardians of the wellspring of life, teaching each generation the importance of sexual purity before marriage and fidelity within marriage.

Today, attitudes toward human sexuality threaten the moral authority of women in many ways. Abortion for convenience destroys a woman's most sacred powers and destroys her moral authority. Sexual immorality and immodesty debase women and reinforce the lie that a woman's sexuality is what defines her worth. Women were once held to a higher standard.

Spiritual and economic poverty grows out of sexual relations without conscience. Unwed mothers often cannot support their children, and the children often grow up in poverty, without the guiding influence of a father. Promiscuity simply robs women of their moral influence and degrades society.

In this way, they have been a civilizing influence in society; they have brought out the best in men; they have perpetuated wholesome environments in which to raise secure and healthy children.

Partnership for Tomorrow

The world often devalues marriage, motherhood and homemaking. There is no question that women are as a group more intelligent, healthier, and more capable than men. They can achieve, accomplish and outdo most men when in direct competition. However, there is no higher good than mothers and fathers in partnership.

Men are not excused from their own duty to stand for truth and righteousness. They, too, have a responsibility to serve, sacrifice, and care for children. Men must stand with women, share their burdens, and support each other.

There is no superior career, and no amount of money, authority, or public acclaim that can exceed the ultimate rewards of family. Do not be afraid to be an influence for good. You do not need to apologize when you teach, correct, challenge, and rear children with love. Teach them to pray, and to be good people.

Women from my childhood, teen years, and adulthood had great influence on my self-confidence, identity and courage. Their influence is felt long after they passed on.

Speech #22

Discerning Truth from Error

Boston College History Class

In a college history class, I was aggressively taught that Social Darwinism, Imperialism and Marxist Socialism evolved from revolution and the struggle of the exploited masses taking power from the few rich. I believed that America's great purpose is to provide not only religious freedom, but also opportunity to acquire wealth and prosperity.

Most students in my class believed that this was no longer possible. They believed that the 'establishment' had gobbled up all wealth and power for themselves. It was ironic that most of these young men and women came from very wealthy families. It seemed that some students almost despised their "capitalistic" parents. Ironically, after graduation, most of the young men shaved their beards and long hair and replaced their beads with a tie and business attire. They followed their parents and quickly became what they had called "capitalist pigs."

Adam Smith Model

During one study session, I boldly said, "My father was a farmer and a teacher. I came from a poor, hard-working family, but I believe that if I study and work hard I can be rich, famous and powerful." When they told me that I was dreaming, I said that they would probably appreciate their education a lot more if they had to pay for it like I did, and not just have it handed to them on a silver platter. That evoked some critical reactions. Our assistant professor then suggested that I represent the Adam

Smith view because of the way I viewed things. At the time, I didn't really understand who Adam Smith was, but I believed in the American Dream. He was a Scottish 1770 author of the well-respected book titled The Wealth of Nations addressing factors such as perpetuating wealth or poverty, manufacturing, trade, coinage, etc.

Communist Manifesto

In class, someone quoted from our textbook, where it described the rise of the proletariat (the lower working class, or manual labor) to the position of the ruling class, which had wealth and political supremacy. This was to be accomplished by following the steps outlined in Marx's Communist Manifesto. Marx advocated taking money, or capital, from the bourgeoisie (the middle class businessmen) and centralizing all instruments of production in the hands of the government. The blueprint was as follows:

1. Abolition of private property.
2. A heavy progressive or graduated income tax (the more you earn, the more you pay).
3. 3Abolition of all rights of inheritance.
4. Confiscation of the property of all emigrants and rebels.
5. Centralization of credit in the hands of the State (government), by means of a national bank.
6. Centralization of the means of communication and transport by the State.
7. Establishment of industrial armies, etc.

The Russians at the time used this scheme to justify the social revolution taking place in their country. My response in class was, "It is a description of what is happening in our own country. Whether or not it was good for the individual or the nation is another question."

The bell rang and the class was over. I was troubled by the whole spirit of the thing, but I couldn't put my finger on what it was.

Annexation of the Philippines

The next day, as the students gathered in the large amphitheater in McEwen Hall, the professor launched into a subtle attack on America's Imperialistic aggressions. He referred to the following account from an interview with U.S. President William McKinley in 1900 after annexing the Philippine Islands:

"I have been criticized a good deal about the Philippines, but I don't deserve it. The truth is, I didn't want the Philippines, and when they came to us, as a gift from the gods, I did not know what to do with them. When the Spanish war broke out, Dewey was at Hong Kong, and I ordered him to go to Manila, and he had to; because, if defeated, he had no place to refit [repair a ship] on that side of the globe, and if the Dons [the Spanish] were victorious, they would likely cross the Pacific and ravage our Oregon and California coasts. And so he had to destroy the Spanish fleet, and did it.

"But that was as far as I thought then. When next I realized that the Philippines had dropped into our lap, I confess that I did not know what to do with them. I sought counsel from all sides—Democrats as well as Republicans—but got little help. I thought first we would take only Manila; then Luzon; then other islands, perhaps all. I walked the floor of the White House night after night until midnight; and I am not ashamed to tell you, gentlemen, that I went down on my knees and prayed to Almighty God for light and guidance more than one night. And one night late it came to me this way – I don't know how it was, but it came: (1) That we could not give them back to Spain

– that would be cowardly and dishonorable; (2) that we could not turn them over to France or Germany – that would be bad business and discreditable; (3) that we could not leave them to themselves – they were unfit for self-government – and they would soon have anarchy and misrule over there worse than Spain's was; and (4) that there was nothing left for us to do but to take them all, and to educate the Filipinos, and uplift and civilize and Christianize them, and, by God's grace, do the very best we could by them, as our fellowmen for whom Christ died.

"And then I went to bed, and went to sleep, and slept soundly, and next morning I sent for the chief engineer of the War Department (our mapmaker) and told him to put the Philippines on the map of the United States . . . ; and there they are, and there they will stay while I am President!"

Using Religion to Lie

Our professor boldly called President McKinley a liar for saying that God had inspired him. It was at that moment that I knew something terrible was wrong in our class. I raised my hand and was called on to comment. I asked the professor why he thought President McKinley was liar.

He said, "Because there is no God, and he just used that as an excuse to justify to the American people's obvious imperialistic aggression."

I said, "But he may have sincerely believed that he had been inspired. The account impressed me that way. We can't judge him as an intentional liar. Maybe he believed in God, even if you don't."

"Yes," was his response, "Almost all bourgeoisies believe in God. That is how they justify their actions. This is the very evil that is the cause of today's capitalistic imperialism and aggression on the weaker peoples of the world."

I bravely countered, "It sounds to me like you're advocating socialism instead of just teaching us about it."

He responded without reservation. "Yes, I am a socialist and advocate it as the ultimate solution." As he spoke those words, I first felt the cold reality of what he was doing. During the moments that he spoke and those following as he waited for my rebuttal, I felt in my heart the difference between the truth and error of what was being taught. It was then that so many things came into clear focus.

My response was also to the point, "Now I see things much more clearly. I hope the rest of these students can see what you are trying to do. It's one thing to learn about communism and socialism, but it's quite another thing to be taught and convinced that it is better than democracy."

The 125 other students had watched wide-eyed and listened without interruption to our brief debate. After a long silence, the professor asked if he could continue, and he did. When the class was over, I went down and told him that I didn't want to be offensive. (I did not want him to lower my grade because I enjoyed the class!) I added that I felt like I had to comment. He was polite and agreed that it was important that we recognize one another's differences. Since then, I have felt strongly impressed to confirm the truth and call out lies and deceptions.

Note: Socialism is defined as: state (government) ownership of capital and industry. Any of various economic and political philosophies that support social equality, collective decision-making, distribution of income based on contribution, and public, not private, ownership of productive capital and natural resources. Americans must guard against the many federal government programs that the states and individuals should be responsible for. Socialism refers to any benefit we try to get the federal government to do for people that they should do for themselves.

Speech #23

What Makes America Great?

Do I Have a Chance?

"The probability that we may fail in the struggle ought not to deter us from the support of a cause we believe to be just; it shall not deter me."

- Abraham Lincoln

"Miracles start to happen when you give as much energy to your dreams as you do to your fears."

- Anonymous

For This Time

"Who knoweth whether thou art come to the kingdom for such a time as this?"

- Old Testament, Esther 4:14

We were all born for such a time as this. We have a destiny to meet. We reap what we sow, and because we have been given more freedom and more opportunities and privileges, we must do more. One person can make a difference. Each of us has a role to play in preserving our nation. We must make a difference! We must make a difference individually and as a nation.

Good Is Great

The French philosopher Alexis de Tocqueville said,

"I sought for the greatness and genius of America in her . . . fertile fields and boundless prairies, and it was not there; in her rich mines and her vast world commerce and it was not there. Not until I went to the churches of America and heard her pulpits aflame with righteousness did I understand the secret of her genius and power. America is great because she is good, and if America ever ceases to be good, America will cease to be great."

James Madison said, "We have staked the whole future of American civilization not upon the power of government—far from it. We have staked the future . . . upon the capacity of each . . . of us to govern ourselves according to the Ten Commandments of God."

The United States is a great country, and I am so very grateful to be an American. Our greatness is in the goodness of our people. Our true greatness is not in our buildings, our economy, or our technology. It is in our people who love life and liberty. Our Constitution was written by good people for good people. It will survive if we remain good. It will not survive if we continue to lose our moral foundation. If America ceases to be good, America will cease to be great.

Evil Is Wrong

> *"A good man out of the good treasure of the heart bringeth forth good things: and an evil man out of the evil treasure bringeth forth evil things."*
>
> - New Testament, Matthew 12:35

Fraud and misrepresentation create confusion and erode public trust. Immorality and abuse of power destroy personal integrity and weaken our families, our cities, and our nation.

Deception and deceit are evidenced in those who rewrite history and attempt to reinvent religion. Hollywood, Wall

Street, sports arenas and leisure are replacing churches, synagogues, mosques and family gatherings. They are reshaping the American people. There are flagrant violations of integrity in every industry, every arm of government and community. Lying, cheating, stealing and bullying are breaches of trust. There is a resounding assault on the family. Some want to ban the Pledge of Allegiance, prayer or mention of God from any public forum.

These evidences of moral decay and civil decline are alarming. Those who promote this decay and decline either do not understand true principles of freedom or they are evil in their intent.

We Must Be Trustworthy

It was said of George Washington, "He never lied, fudged, or cheated . . . [He] came to stand for the new nation and its republican virtues, which was why he became our first President by unanimous choice."

Trust is a keystone of any relationship and any organization. Trust and faith go hand in hand. Love grows out of trust. We admire those we trust and fear those we don't.

We Must Live with Integrity

George Washington said, "I hope I shall always possess firmness and virtue enough to maintain what I consider the most enviable of all titles, the character of an 'Honest Man.'"

John Adams said, "I had rather you should be worthy possessors of one thousand pounds honestly acquired by your own labor . . . than of ten millions by banks and tricks."

John Adams also said, "I never swerved from any principle . . . to obtain a vote. I never sacrificed a friend or betrayed a trust."

America needs citizens and leaders with integrity. We have integrity when we do what we say we will do. We have integrity when we keep a confidence and when we tell the truth. Our integrity is demonstrated by what we think, what we say and what we do.

> *"I will not remove mine integrity from me. My righteousness I hold fast, and will not let it go."*
> - Old Testament, Job 27:5-6

Abraham Lincoln stated, "I never use any man's money but my own."

When he was just twenty-four years old, Lincoln was appointed postmaster of the New Salem, Illinois, post office. It was closed part way through the year. A postal agent from Washington arrived to retrieve the unused portion of Lincoln's salary. Lincoln retrieved the unused $17 of the $55.70 annual salary from a trunk. It was in a yellow rag, tied with a string. The agent was stunned. He had not expected to find such integrity in a simple man.

We too can be honest. We all want to be dealt with honestly. This is a critical part of the foundation of society.

Serve Others without Expectation

In 1777, John Adams to Abigail Adams: "You will never know how much it cost [our] generation to preserve your freedom. I hope you will make good use of it! If you do not, I shall repent in Heaven that I ever took half the pains to preserve it!"

There are opportunities to serve all around us. We can help others along their way. Service is fundamental to any relationship, community or nation. We must be on higher ground if we intend to help lift others up. This is selfless service I am describing. It is not forced or coerced service. The most important service is with family, friends and neighbors. For now, I must leave it to your imagination and to your efforts to plan and execute such service.

Strengthen Your Family and Home

> *"I believe our problems, almost every one, arise out of the homes of the people. If there is to be a reformation, if there is to be a change, if there is to be a return to old and sacred values, it must begin in the home. It is here that truth is learned; that integrity is cultivated, that self-discipline is instilled, and that love is nurtured . . . It is in the home that we learn the values by which we guide our lives. That home may be ever so simple . . . but with a good father and a good mother, it can become a place of wondrous upbringing . . . It is broken homes that lead to a breakup in society."*
>
> - Gordon B. Hinckley

If the family fails, our lives are impacted and our nation weakened. The family is the nest in which to nurture. It is the classroom in which to teach and where to set the example and character model of personal virtues and qualities of greatness.

Nothing can take the place of a mother and father who demonstrate fidelity to one another and who are dedicated to rearing happy, disciplined and educated children. The church can support the family. The school can support the family. The community can support the family. It is the family that teaches and strengthens personal values, supports personal responsibility and cultivates mature contributing adults. But, it is the family that will rear the generation to strengthen the nation and insure the future.

The family is where we begin to recognize our individual identity and self-worth. It is where we receive our spiritual, emotional and patriotic imprint. It is the source of love, courage and patriotism. If you are not strengthening your family, you are weakening our nation.

Divine Intervention

> *"No people can be bound to acknowledge and adore the invisible hand, which conducts the affairs of men, more than the People of the United States. Every step . . . seems to have been distinguished by some token of providential agency."*
>
> - Washington's First Inaugural Address

Patrick Henry stated, "There is a just God who presides over the destinies of nations, and who will raise up friends to fight our battles for us."

There was no question in the minds of the early settlers and colonists that God was supporting what they were doing. It was not just a customary thing to do, but a necessary thing to seek His guidance and help.

Patriots Revolted

> *"They were out manned, outmaneuvered, outsmarted, and outgunned again and again by a superior British army. Yet they prevailed. Surely the only explanation is the intervention of God."*
>
> - Sheri Dew

The colonial society and economy developed, along with the recognition of a need for representation and a desire for independence. Planted throughout the country were men and women of greatness who incubated innovation, ideals, visions of expansion, and the love of liberty.

As events occurred and decisions were made, the spirit of revolution was lit in the hearts of Patriots. They began the difficult task of throwing off the yoke of British rule. The Declaration of Independence was written and promoted, and a most important fight for freedom began.

Battles were fought, sacrifices were made and blood was spilled. Through a long and terrible struggle, truth and freedom prevailed. The Redcoats returned back to England. Wounds healed, the dead were buried, and Americans returned to their families and farms or other industries.

The Articles of Confederation Gave Most of the Power to the States

After the British surrender at Yorktown, Virginia, in 1881, the fighting mostly ended. The states struggled with their new-found freedom. The Founding Fathers met and agreed to continue government under the Articles of Confederation, with some adjustments. State delegates ratified the revised document, and the Articles, originally written at the beginning of war, were the law of the new country for six years.

Because of a wide-spread distrust of a potential king or strong central government, the Articles gave most of the power to the states. Each state made its own laws, collected its own taxes, and printed its own money. The Congress of the federal government had little power to enforce the laws it passed for the country. It did establish rules for expanding the territory of the country and adding new states. It established international relationships. It was also financially broke.

Over the next few years, the thirteen states wrote their own state constitutions and set up their own state governments. It was inevitable, however, that there would be conflict between the people of different states.

In 1788, another Constitutional Convention was called, and the best men of the land gathered to frame a document that would help solve the political problems of the country. This would be a government like no other ever framed. It would bind the states together, give them the power to make many of their own laws and policies, and control the power of a national government. At the same time, representatives from all the states would make up a Congress that would vote on laws for the whole country. The national government was given powers it needed to provide defense with an army and a navy, make treaties with foreign countries, appoint judges to courts, operate a national postal system, make coins determine the value of money, and make sure laws were carried out.

In 1787, May through September, delegates from the thirteen states met in Philadelphia, where they debated and argued about principle and process. There were many challenges and obstacles to overcome, but they worked tirelessly to bring about a miracle.

The Founders Looked to God

During the hottest days of the summer, the men found themselves in gridlock. Issues of representation and property were hotly contested. James Madison recorded that the wise and venerable Ben Franklin acknowledged their "imperfection of human understanding" . . . and "want of political wisdom." They had studied ancient and modern governments, none of which were totally suitable for America.

Franklin admitted that they were "groping as it were in the dark to find political truth" and pointed out that they had not asked God for light and understanding. He went on to remind everyone that during the Revolutionary War they "had daily prayers" that were "graciously answered," and he asked everyone if they had "forgotten that powerful friend" or if "we imagine that we no longer need His assistance?"

Then he testified of the convincing truth that, "God governs in the affairs of men. And if a sparrow cannot fall to the ground without His notice, is it probable that an empire can rise without his aid?" He then warned the group that the Bible warned that "except the Lord build the House, they labor in vain that build it;" Psalms 127:1.

Franklin moved, "that henceforth prayers imploring the assistance of Heaven, and its blessings on our deliberations, be held in this Assembly every morning before we proceed to business." There was some debate on the motion, but beginning the next morning of July 4th, prayers were offered throughout the rest of the convention.

The Constitution itself was revolutionary and visionary, with promises to future generations. It became the supreme law of the land when it was ratified by nine states in 1789. The last of the thirteen states finally ratified it in 1790. The Constitution was the most significant legislative document ever written and adopted by any people. It "exceeded the genius" of all the delegates combined, and proved to be a work of men inspired of God.

We Must Look to God

Today, more than ever before, we must look to God for guidance, strength and protection. Perhaps in a relative sense, we are weaker and more vulnerable now than the Patriots were at the time of the signing of the Declaration of Independence or the colonists were just before the ratification of the U.S. Constitution.

Today, we cannot become intoxicated with our wealth or influence in the world. We cannot be arrogant and believe that we prosper because of our own genius. We cannot think we are so important and sophisticated that we can forget God or do not need Him.

> *"The . . . smiles of heaven can never be expected on a nation that disregards the eternal rules of order and right, which heaven itself has ordained."*
>
> - George Washington

> *"We are forgetting God, whose commandments we have put aside. . . . In all too many ways we have substituted human sophistry for the wisdom of the Almighty. . . . Can we expect peace and prosperity . . . while turning our backs on the source of our strength?"*
>
> - Gordon B. Hinckley

A Modern Civil War

We find ourselves in a polarized world torn between good and evil. The signs of the times are evident. Our country is divided over a multitude of serious issues. Ours is a "civil" war dividing families and communities. The battle is not being waged with cannon, muskets or bayonets, but with economics, law, technology, hate, sin and intolerance.

A significant part of this war has to do with whether God can continue to play a role in our private and public lives or not. There are many people, citing the division of church and state, who want to take prayer out of schools, courtrooms, and any other public forum. They want to stop or change the Pledge of Allegiance because God is included. They want "IN GOD WE TRUST" taken off our coins. This civil war must not continue. We cannot let this happen. We are one nation under God. God bless America, and God bless the American people.

Speech #24

Who I Am, and My Goals as President

It is my honor and privilege to speak to you today. We all want to be well thought of and to be accepted; I am no different. I hope to win over your hearts and minds so you will like me, support me and vote for me.

Some of you may be saying to yourself, "That's not going to happen!" However, I do have a message that I believe will resonate with you and that you will be excited to receive and act on.

Before I deliver the message, permit me to tell you a little about the messenger.

First, I am a Mormon and a member of The Church of Jesus Christ of Latter-day Saints. Some of you may have been told, and even believe, that I belong to a cult. To address that concern, I can only testify that is not true in any way. Like other members of this church, I know God lives and that His son Jesus Christ is the Savior of the world. He has changed my life and I have been born again. I am His disciple and want to follow Him.

Second. I've not held public office before, and I'm not a practicing attorney. However, I have studied law, and I understand the Constitution. I'm not a veteran, a wealthy man, nor a famous movie personality. I do love America and I understand business. I have the heart of a teacher, and I have spent a lot of my life in service.

My Goal as President

I don't want to be remembered as the president who won World War III or stimulated the economy with creative programs. I do want to be the president who keeps us out of war and gets us out of debt. I want to balance the budget and stabilize our currency so the free market can heal itself. I want to help repeal the 16th Amendment— to repeal the graduated income tax and replace it with a flat tax. I also want to help repeal the 17th Amendment—to bring back election of Senators to state legislatures, which gives more power to those state-elected groups.

I am very concerned that our religious liberties are slowly being undermined and eroded away. On the other hand, there are also some who knowingly or unknowingly use Christianity as their rationale to use government to force others to pay for medical care, food, housing, and many other economic helps that are not constitutionally appropriate. They claim we are not true Christians if we are not willing to use federal tax dollars to provide for the poor. In either case and regardless of their rationale, this is not right. It is not constitutional, nor does it pass the test of separation of church and state.

These modern-day crusaders are using force to accomplish their purposes. In doing so, they are willingly giving up personal liberty. By establishing a welfare state, we are setting up a state church. Instead, we must let voluntary personal, church, and charity services and contributions help alleviate society's economic problems and pull the poor up to where they can provide for themselves.

It is my goal to bring an end to foreign entanglements and unconstitutional wars. It is not the role nor the destiny of America to build up nations or police the world. We have enough problems here at home to keep us busy and to use all of our resources. It is not our job to "protect our national interests" abroad because we do not own, nor deserve to control, the resources of other countries.

We should protect our national interest at home by utilizing our natural resources here first, and then purchasing those we need at a fair market value. Let us develop businesses and products and jobs here first. Fair market value will be fair if we compete in the world marketplace while taking care of business at home first.

Our Future

We will have great opportunities in the future if we are doing what we should do as a nation. If we as a nation work hard and are honest, we will achieve. If we as a nation are good and do what is right, we will be protected and we will prosper.

The problems of our country are easily understood and the answers to them are not that difficult. Abusing the rule of law and ignoring the Constitution can be reversed. We must once again endorse a system of self-reliance, personal responsibility, sound money, and a non-interventionist foreign policy. We must reject and change the cradle-to-grave nanny state. This is the right direction for the United States of America.

It's my hope that you will learn more about me by reading my literature and studying the Constitution, and then choose to be actively involved in my campaign. Regardless of what you decide, be assured that I respect you and your opinions. I ask God to bless you and your family.

Speech #25

My Personal Values

God created this world. He has given us inalienable rights. He has assisted in righteous causes and blessed righteous people throughout history, but He does not ignore the agency of mankind to choose their ideals and actions.

America is a blessed land. This land was preserved and prepared as a cradle of freedom by divine providence. It was difficult to achieve freedom, and it will be a struggle to preserve it. If Americans are righteous, they will prosper, be blessed, and remain free. History is the result of the choices made by others who have gone before us. The future will be a result of our choices. It is necessary and good to protect life, liberty and property. The United States of America is sovereign and stands separate from all other nations.

The Declaration of Independence and the United States Constitution were inspired of God. God raised up and supported the Founding Fathers who expressed their grievances, declared independence, fought for liberty and drafted and accepted the standard of liberty for the world. There is wisdom in not straying from the original intent and text of the U.S. Constitution. It was intended to limit the role and power of the federal government. There have been changes that have weakened the Constitution. Every citizen must defend, protect and preserve this sacred document.

Governments and law are essential. Governments are instituted of God for the benefit of man. When unchecked, most individuals and governments abuse power. God will hold those in power accountable for their acts in relationship to making and administering laws for the good and safety of society. Governments have the right to enact laws to secure the public interest while protecting each individual's free exercise of conscience and religious belief, the right to control property, and to protect life. Crimes should be punished according to the nature of the offense.

Governments and citizens have sacred duties and responsibilities. Public service is a sacred honor and responsibility requiring sacrifice and allegiance. Public officials must enforce the law and administer justice as they uphold the voice of the people. Citizens are bound to obey the laws of the land and sustain and uphold the government that protects them. It is not right to mingle religious influence with civil government in order to favor one religious society over another. However, it is right—and even essential—to include righteous influence and discussion in government. Citizens should seek out and support honest, wise, trustworthy, and moral people to serve in public office. Our country and its citizens should be examples of strength and freedom, personal liberty, and inspire other nations to be like us instead of trying to coerce them to be like us.

There are evil powers trying to destroy liberty. Throughout the history of the world, there have been those who have tried to destroy liberty. This struggle between good and evil continues today. Citizens must watch for dangers and guard against those evil people and groups whose purpose is to get power and punish those not of their religion or ideology. They are among us, or will come among us, and we must warn others. If America becomes wicked, it will lose its freedom and be destroyed.

I am for good and against evil. I am for freedom and against slavery. I am for social progress and against socialism. I am for a dynamic economy and against waste. I am for the private competitive market and against unnecessary government intervention. I am for national security and against appeasement and capitulation to an obvious enemy. I am more for individual rights and responsibilities, free market, respect for equality, a strong military and believe America is the best!

"I am pro-liberty, pro-freedom, pro-local self-government, and pro-everything else that has made us the free country we have grown to be. It necessarily follows that I am anti-internationalist, anti-interventionist, anti-meddlesome-busy-bodiness in our international affairs. In the domestic field, I am anti-socialist, anti-communist, anti-welfare state."

- Anonymous

"You cannot bring about prosperity by discouraging thrift. You cannot strengthen the weak by weakening the strong. You cannot help the wage earner by pulling down the wage payer. You cannot further the brotherhood of man by encouraging class hatred. You cannot help the poor by destroying the rich. You cannot solve problems by spending more than you earn. You cannot build character and courage by taking away a person's initiative and independence. You cannot help people permanently by doing for them what they could and should do for themselves."

- Anonymous

Epilogue

So many patriots through the years have given us hope and vision. They have given us sound principles, including individual rights and the rule of law. They have given us the Constitution of the United States of America. They have given us a nation and society in which we have blossomed and flourished.

We now have the opportunity to stand on their shoulders and give a better world to generations that follow. It is my desire and prayer that we will do so.

In summary, I wish to leave you with the lesson taught in the following poem title *The Bridge Builder* by Will Allen Dromgoole.

An old man going a lone highway,
Came at the evening, cold and gray,
To a chasm, vast, and deep and wide,
Through which was flowing a sullen tide.
The old man crossed in the twilight dim;
The sullen stream had no fear for him;
But he turned, when safe on the other side,
And built a bridge to span the tide.

"Old man," said a fellow pilgrim, near,
"You are wasting strength with building here;
Your journey will end with the ending day;

You never again will pass this way;
You've crossed the chasm, deep and wide-
Why build you this bridge at the evening tide?"

The builder lifted his old gray head;
"Good friend, in the path I have come," he said,
"There followeth after me today,
A youth, whose feet must pass this way.

This chasm, that has been naught to me,
To that fair-haired youth may a pitfall be.
He, too, must cross in the twilight dim;
Good friend, I am building this bridge for him."

Resources

Appendix A

Declaration of Independence

IN CONGRESS, July 4, 1776.

The unanimous Declaration of the thirteen united States of America.

When in the Course of human events, it becomes necessary for one people to dissolve the political bands which have connected them with another, and to assume among the powers of the earth, the separate and equal station to which the Laws of Nature and of Nature's God entitle them, a decent respect to the opinions of mankind requires that they should declare the causes which impel them to the separation.

We hold these truths to be self-evident, that all men are created equal, that they are endowed by their Creator with certain unalienable Rights, that among these are Life, Liberty and the pursuit of Happiness.--That to secure these rights, Governments are instituted among Men, deriving their just powers from the consent of the governed, --That whenever any Form of Government becomes destructive of these ends, it is the Right of the People to alter or to abolish it, and to institute new Government, laying its foundation on such principles and organizing its powers in such form, as to them shall seem most likely to effect their Safety and Happiness. Prudence, indeed, will dictate that Governments long established should not be changed for light and transient causes; and accordingly all experience hath shewn, that mankind are more disposed to suffer, while evils are sufferable, than to right themselves by abolishing the forms to which they are accustomed. But when a long train of abuses and usurpations, pursuing invariably the same Object evinces a design to reduce them under absolute Despotism, it is their right, it is their duty, to throw off such Government, and to provide new Guards for their future security.--Such has been the patient sufferance of these Colonies; and such is now the necessity which constrains them to alter their former Systems of Government. The history of the present King of Great Britain is a history of repeated injuries and usurpations, all having in direct object the establishment of an absolute Tyranny over these States. To prove this, let Facts be submitted to a candid world.

He has refused his Assent to Laws, the most wholesome and necessary for the public good.

He has forbidden his Governors to pass Laws of immediate and pressing importance, unless suspended in their operation till his Assent should be obtained; and when so suspended, he has utterly neglected to attend to them.

He has refused to pass other Laws for the accommodation of large districts of people, unless those people would relinquish the right of Representation in the Legislature, a right inestimable to them and formidable to tyrants only.

He has called together legislative bodies at places unusual, uncomfortable, and distant from the depository of their public Records, for the sole purpose of fatiguing them into compliance with his measures.

He has dissolved Representative Houses repeatedly, for opposing with manly firmness his invasions on the rights of the people.

He has refused for a long time, after such dissolutions, to cause others to be elected; whereby the Legislative powers, incapable of Annihilation, have returned to the People at large for their exercise; the State remaining in the mean time exposed to all the dangers of invasion from without, and convulsions within.

He has endeavoured to prevent the population of these States; for that purpose obstructing the Laws for Naturalization of Foreigners; refusing to pass others to encourage their migrations hither, and raising the conditions of new Appropriations of Lands.

He has obstructed the Administration of Justice, by refusing his Assent to Laws for establishing Judiciary powers.

He has made Judges dependent on his Will alone, for the tenure of their offices, and the amount and payment of their salaries.

He has erected a multitude of New Offices, and sent hither swarms of Officers to harrass our people, and eat out their substance.

He has kept among us, in times of peace, Standing Armies without the Consent of our legislatures.

He has affected to render the Military independent of and superior to the Civil power.

He has combined with others to subject us to a jurisdiction foreign to our constitution, and unacknowledged by our laws; giving his Assent to their Acts of pretended Legislation:

For Quartering large bodies of armed troops among us:

For protecting them, by a mock Trial, from punishment for any Murders which they should commit on the Inhabitants of these States:

For cutting off our Trade with all parts of the world:

For imposing Taxes on us without our Consent:

For depriving us in many cases, of the benefits of Trial by Jury:

For transporting us beyond Seas to be tried for pretended offences

For abolishing the free System of English Laws in a neighbouring Province, establishing therein an Arbitrary government, and enlarging its Boundaries so as to render it at once an example and fit instrument for introducing the same absolute rule into these Colonies:

For taking away our Charters, abolishing our most valuable Laws, and altering fundamentally the Forms of our Governments:

For suspending our own Legislatures, and declaring themselves invested with power to legislate for us in all cases whatsoever.

He has abdicated Government here, by declaring us out of his Protection and waging War against us.

He has plundered our seas, ravaged our Coasts, burnt our towns, and destroyed the lives of our people.

He is at this time transporting large Armies of foreign Mercenaries to compleat the works of death, desolation and tyranny, already begun with circumstances of Cruelty & perfidy scarcely paralleled in the most barbarous ages, and totally unworthy the Head of a civilized nation.

He has constrained our fellow Citizens taken Captive on the high Seas to bear Arms against their Country, to become the executioners of their friends and Brethren, or to fall themselves by their Hands.

He has excited domestic insurrections amongst us, and has endeavoured to bring on the inhabitants of our frontiers, the merciless Indian Savages, whose known rule of warfare, is an undistinguished destruction of all ages, sexes and conditions.

In every stage of these Oppressions We have Petitioned for Redress in the most humble terms: Our repeated Petitions have been answered only by repeated injury. A Prince whose character is thus marked by every act which may define a Tyrant, is unfit to be the ruler of a free people.

Nor have We been wanting in attentions to our Brittish brethren. We have warned them from time to time of attempts by their legislature to extend an unwarrantable jurisdiction over us. We have reminded them of the circumstances of our emigration and settlement here. We have appealed to their native justice and magnanimity, and we have conjured them by the ties of our common kindred to disavow these usurpations, which, would inevitably interrupt our connections and correspondence. They too have been deaf to the voice of justice and of consanguinity. We must, therefore, acquiesce in the necessity, which denounces our Separation, and hold them, as we hold the rest of mankind, Enemies in War, in Peace Friends.

We, therefore, the Representatives of the united States of America, in General Congress, Assembled, appealing to the Supreme Judge of the world for the rectitude of our intentions, do, in the Name, and by Authority of the good People of these Colonies, solemnly publish and declare, That these United Colonies are, and of Right ought to be Free and Independent States; that they are Absolved from all Allegiance to the British Crown, and that all political connection between them and the State of Great Britain, is and ought to be totally dissolved; and that as Free and Independent States, they have full Power to levy War, conclude Peace, contract Alliances, establish Commerce, and to do all other Acts and Things which Independent States may of right do. And for the support of this Declaration, with a firm reliance on the protection of divine Providence, we mutually pledge to each other our Lives, our Fortunes and our sacred Honor.

The 56 signatures on the Declaration appear in the positions indicated:

Column 1
- Georgia:
  - Button Gwinnett
  - Lyman Hall
  - George Walton

Column 2
- North Carolina:
  - William Hooper
  - Joseph Hewes
  - John Penn
- South Carolina:
  - Edward Rutledge
  - Thomas Heyward, Jr.
  - Thomas Lynch, Jr.
  - Arthur Middleton

Column 3
- Massachusetts:
  - John Hancock
- Maryland:
  - Samuel Chase
  - William Paca
  - Thomas Stone
  - Charles Carroll of Carrollton
- Virginia:
  - George Wythe
  - Richard Henry Lee
  - Thomas Jefferson
  - Benjamin Harrison
  - Thomas Nelson, Jr.
  - Francis Lightfoot Lee
  - Carter Braxton

Column 4
- Pennsylvania:
  - Robert Morris
  - Benjamin Rush
  - Benjamin Franklin
  - John Morton
  - George Clymer
  - James Smith
  - George Taylor
  - James Wilson
  - George Ross
- Delaware
  - Caesar Rodney
  - George Read
  - Thomas McKean

Column 5
- New York
  - William Floyd
  - Philip Livingston
  - Francis Lewis
  - Lewis Morris
- New Jersey
  - Richard Stockton
  - John Witherspoon
  - Francis Hopkinson
  - John Hart
  - Abraham Clark

Column 6
- New Hampshire
  - Josiah Bartlett
  - William Whipple
- Massachusetts
  - Samuel Adams
  - John Adams
  - Robert Treat Paine
  - Elbridge Gerry
- Rhode Island
  - Stephen Hopkins
  - William Ellery
- Connecticut
  - Roger Sherman
  - Samuel Huntington
  - William Williams
  - Oliver Wolcott
- New Hampshire
  - Matthew Thornton

Appendix B

Constitution of the United States

Here is the complete text of the U.S. Constitution. The original spelling and capitalization have been retained.

We the People of the United States, in Order to form a more perfect Union, establish Justice, insure domestic Tranquility, provide for the common defense, promote the general Welfare, and secure the Blessings of Liberty to ourselves and our Posterity, do ordain and establish this Constitution for the United States of America.

Article I

Section 1.

All legislative Powers herein granted shall be vested in a Congress of the United States, which shall consist of a Senate and House of Representatives.

Section 2.

The House of Representatives shall be composed of Members chosen every second Year by the People of the several States, and the Electors in each State shall have the Qualifications requisite for Electors of the most numerous Branch of the State Legislature.

No Person shall be a Representative who shall not have attained to the age of twenty five Years, and been seven Years a Citizen of the United States, and who shall not, when elected, be an Inhabitant of that State in which he shall be chosen.

Representatives and direct Taxes shall be apportioned among the several States which may be included within this Union, according to their respective Numbers, which shall be determined by adding to the whole Number of free Persons, including those bound to Service for a Term of Years, and excluding Indians not taxed, three fifths of all other Persons. The actual Enumeration shall be made within three Years after the first Meeting of the Congress of the United States, and within every subsequent Term of ten Years, in such Manner as they shall by Law direct. The Number of Representatives shall not exceed one for every thirty Thousand, but each State shall have at Least one Representative; and until such enumeration shall be made, the State of New Hampshire shall be entitled to chuse three, Massachusetts eight, Rhode-Island and Providence Plantations one, Connecticut five, New-York six, New Jersey four, Pennsylvania eight, Delaware one, Maryland six, Virginia ten, North Carolina five, South Carolina five, and Georgia three.

When vacancies happen in the Representation from any State, the Executive Authority thereof shall issue Writs of Election to fill such Vacancies.

The House of Representatives shall chuse their Speaker and other Officers; and shall have the sole Power of Impeachment.

Section 3.

The Senate of the United States shall be composed of two Senators from each State, chosen by the Legislature thereof, for six Years; and each Senator shall have one Vote.

Immediately after they shall be assembled in Consequence of the first Election, they shall be divided as equally as may be into three Classes. The Seats of the Senators of the first Class shall be vacated at the Expiration of the second Year, of the second Class at the Expiration of the fourth Year, and the third Class at the Expiration of the sixth Year, so that one third may be chosen every second Year; and if Vacancies happen by Resignation, or otherwise, during the Recess of the Legislature of any State, the Executive thereof may make temporary Appointments until the next Meeting of the Legislature, which shall then fill such Vacancies.

No Person shall be a Senator who shall not have attained to the Age of thirty Years, and

been nine Years a Citizen of the United States and who shall not, when elected, be an Inhabitant of that State for which he shall be chosen.
The Vice President of the United States shall be President of the Senate, but shall have no Vote, unless they be equally divided.
The Senate shall chuse their other Officers, and also a President pro tempore, in the Absence of the Vice President, or when he shall exercise the Office of President of the United States.
The Senate shall have the sole Power to try all Impeachments. When sitting for that Purpose, they shall be on Oath or Affirmation. When the President of the United States is tried, the Chief Justice shall preside: And no Person shall be convicted without the Concurrence of two thirds of the Members present.
Judgment in Cases of Impeachment shall not extend further than to removal from Office, and disqualification to hold and enjoy any Office of Honor, Trust or Profit under the United States: but the Party convicted shall nevertheless be liable and subject to Indictment, Trial, Judgment and Punishment, according to Law.

Section 4.
The Times, Places and Manner of holding Elections for Senators and Representatives, shall be prescribed in each State by the Legislature thereof; but the Congress may at any time by Law make or alter such Regulations, except as to the Places of chusing Senators.
The Congress shall assemble at least once in every Year, and such Meeting shall be on the first Monday in December, unless they shall by Law appoint a different Day.

Section 5.
Each House shall be the Judge of the Elections, Returns and Qualifications of its own Members, and a Majority of each shall constitute a Quorum to do Business; but a smaller Number may adjourn from day to day, and may be authorized to compel the Attendance of absent Members, in such Manner, and under such Penalties as each House may provide.
Each House may determine the Rules of its Proceedings, punish its Members for disorderly Behaviour, and, with the Concurrence of two thirds, expel a Member.
Each House shall keep a Journal of its Proceedings, and from time to time publish the same, excepting such Parts as may in their Judgment require Secrecy; and the Yeas and Nays of the Members of either House on any question shall, at the Desire of one fifth of those Present, be entered on the Journal.
Neither House, during the Session of Congress, shall, without the Consent of the other, adjourn for more than three days, nor to any other Place than that in which the two Houses shall be sitting.

Section 6.
The Senators and Representatives shall receive a Compensation for their Services, to be ascertained by Law, and paid out of the Treasury of the United States. They shall in all Cases, except Treason, Felony and Breach of the Peace, be privileged from Arrest during their Attendance at the Session of their respective Houses, and in going to and returning from the same; and for any Speech or Debate in either House, they shall not be questioned in any other Place.
No Senator or Representative shall, during the Time for which he was elected, be appointed to any civil Office under the Authority of the United States, which shall have been created, or the Emoluments whereof shall have been encreased during such time: and no Person holding any Office under the United States, shall be a Member of either House during his Continuance in Office.

Section 7.
All Bills for raising Revenue shall originate in the House of Representatives; but the Senate may propose or concur with Amendments as on other Bills.
Every Bill which shall have passed the House of Representatives and the Senate, shall, before it become a Law, be presented to the President of the United States; if he approve he shall sign it, but if not he shall return it, with his Objections to that House in which it shall have originated, who shall enter the Objections at large on their Journal, and proceed to reconsider it. If after such Reconsideration two thirds of that House shall

agree to pass the Bill, it shall be sent, together with the Objections, to the other House, by which it shall likewise be reconsidered, and if approved by two thirds of that House, it shall become a Law. But in all such Cases the Votes of both Houses shall be determined by Yeas and Nays, and the Names of the Persons voting for and against the Bill shall be entered on the Journal of each House respectively. If any Bill shall not be returned by the President within ten Days (Sundays excepted) after it shall have been presented to him, the Same shall be a Law, in like Manner as if he had signed it, unless the Congress by their Adjournment prevent its Return, in which Case it shall not be a Law.

Every Order, Resolution, or Vote to which the Concurrence of the Senate and House of Representatives may be necessary (except on a question of Adjournment) shall be presented to the President of the United States; and before the Same shall take Effect, shall be approved by him, or being disapproved by him, shall be repassed by two thirds of the Senate and House of Representatives, according to the Rules and Limitations prescribed in the Case of a Bill.

Section 8.

The Congress shall have Power To lay and collect Taxes, Duties, Imposts and Excises, to pay the Debts and provide for the common Defence and general Welfare of the United States; but all Duties, Imposts and Excises shall be uniform throughout the United States;

To borrow Money on the credit of the United States;

To regulate Commerce with foreign Nations, and among the several States, and with the Indian Tribes;

To establish an uniform Rule of Naturalization, and uniform Laws on the subject of Bankruptcies throughout the United States;

To coin Money, regulate the Value thereof, and of foreign Coin, and fix the Standard of Weights and Measures;

To provide for the Punishment of counterfeiting the Securities and current Coin of the United States;

To establish Post Offices and post Roads;

To promote the Progress of Science and useful Arts, by securing for limited Times to Authors and Inventors the exclusive Right to their respective Writings and Discoveries;

To constitute Tribunals inferior to the supreme Court;

To define and punish Piracies and Felonies committed on the high Seas, and Offences against the Law of Nations;

To declare War, grant Letters of Marque and Reprisal, and make Rules concerning Captures on Land and Water;

To raise and support Armies, but no Appropriation of Money to that Use shall be for a longer Term than two Years;

To provide and maintain a Navy;

To make Rules for the Government and Regulation of the land and naval Forces;

To provide for calling forth the Militia to execute the Laws of the Union, suppress Insurrections and repel Invasions;

To provide for organizing, arming, and disciplining, the Militia, and for governing such Part of them as may be employed in the Service of the United States, reserving to the States respectively, the Appointment of the Officers, and the Authority of training the Militia according to the discipline prescribed by Congress;

To exercise exclusive Legislation in all Cases whatsoever, over such District (not exceeding ten Miles square) as may, by Cession of particular States, and the Acceptance of Congress, become the Seat of the Government of the United States, and to exercise like Authority over all Places purchased by the Consent of the Legislature of the State in which the Same shall be, for the Erection of Forts, Magazines, Arsenals, dock-Yards, and other needful Buildings;--And

To make all Laws which shall be necessary and proper for carrying into Execution the foregoing Powers, and all other Powers vested by this Constitution in the Government of the United States, or in any Department or Officer thereof.

Section 9.

The Migration or Importation of such Persons as any of the States now existing shall think proper to admit, shall not be prohibited by the Congress prior to the Year one

thousand eight hundred and eight, but a Tax or duty may be imposed on such Importation, not exceeding ten dollars for each Person.
The Privilege of the Writ of Habeas Corpus shall not be suspended, unless when in Cases of Rebellion or Invasion the public Safety may require it.
No Bill of Attainder or ex post facto Law shall be passed.
No Capitation, or other direct, Tax shall be laid, unless in Proportion to the Census or Enumeration herein before directed to be taken.
No Tax or Duty shall be laid on Articles exported from any State.
No Preference shall be given by any Regulation of Commerce or Revenue to the Ports of one State over those of another: nor shall Vessels bound to, or from, one State, be obliged to enter, clear or pay Duties in another.
No Money shall be drawn from the Treasury, but in Consequence of Appropriations made by Law; and a regular Statement and Account of Receipts and Expenditures of all public Money shall be published from time to time.
No Title of Nobility shall be granted by the United States: And no Person holding any Office of Profit or Trust under them, shall, without the Consent of the Congress, accept of any present, Emolument, Office, or Title, of any kind whatever, from any King, Prince, or foreign State.

Section 10.
No State shall enter into any Treaty, Alliance, or Confederation; grant Letters of Marque and Reprisal; coin Money; emit Bills of Credit; make any Thing but gold and silver Coin a Tender in Payment of Debts; pass any Bill of Attainder, ex post facto Law, or Law impairing the Obligation of Contracts, or grant any Title of Nobility.
No State shall, without the Consent of the Congress, lay any Imposts or Duties on Imports or Exports, except what may be absolutely necessary for executing it's inspection Laws: and the net Produce of all Duties and Imposts, laid by any State on Imports or Exports, shall be for the Use of the Treasury of the United States; and all such Laws shall be subject to the Revision and Controul of the Congress.
No State shall, without the Consent of Congress, lay any Duty of Tonnage, keep Troops, or Ships of War in time of Peace, enter into any Agreement or Compact with another State, or with a foreign Power, or engage in War, unless actually invaded, or in such imminent Danger as will not admit of delay.

Article II

Section 1.
The executive Power shall be vested in a President of the United States of America. He shall hold his Office during the Term of four Years, and, together with the Vice President, chosen for the same Term, be elected, as follows:
Each State shall appoint, in such Manner as the Legislature thereof may direct, a Number of Electors, equal to the whole Number of Senators and Representatives to which the State may be entitled in the Congress: but no Senator or Representative, or Person holding an Office of Trust or Profit under the United States, shall be appointed an Elector.
The Electors shall meet in their respective States, and vote by Ballot for two Persons, of whom one at least shall not be an Inhabitant of the same State with themselves. And they shall make a List of all the Persons voted for, and of the Number of Votes for each; which List they shall sign and certify, and transmit sealed to the Seat of the Government of the United States, directed to the President of the Senate. The President of the Senate shall, in the Presence of the Senate and House of Representatives, open all the Certificates, and the Votes shall then be counted. The Person having the greatest Number of Votes shall be the President, if such Number be a Majority of the whole Number of Electors appointed; and if there be more than one who have such Majority, and have an equal Number of Votes, then the House of Representatives shall immediately chuse by Ballot one of them for President; and if no Person have a Majority, then from the five highest on the List the said House shall in like Manner chuse the President. But in chusing the President, the Votes shall be taken by States, the Representation from each State having one Vote; A quorum for this Purpose shall consist of a Member or Members from two thirds of the States, and a Majority of all the States shall be necessary to a Choice. In

every Case, after the Choice of the President, the Person having the greatest Number of Votes of the Electors shall be the Vice President. But if there should remain two or more who have equal Votes, the Senate shall chuse from them by Ballot the Vice President.

The Congress may determine the Time of chusing the Electors, and the Day on which they shall give their Votes; which Day shall be the same throughout the United States.

No Person except a natural born Citizen, or a Citizen of the United States, at the time of the Adoption of this Constitution, shall be eligible to the Office of President; neither shall any Person be eligible to that Office who shall not have attained to the Age of thirty five Years, and been fourteen Years a Resident within the United States.

In Case of the Removal of the President from Office, or of his Death, Resignation, or Inability to discharge the Powers and Duties of the said Office, the Same shall devolve on the Vice President, and the Congress may by Law provide for the Case of Removal, Death, Resignation or Inability, both of the President and Vice President, declaring what Officer shall then act as President, and such Officer shall act accordingly, until the Disability be removed, or a President shall be elected.

The President shall, at stated Times, receive for his Services, a Compensation, which shall neither be encreased nor diminished during the Period for which he shall have been elected, and he shall not receive within that Period any other Emolument from the United States, or any of them.

Before he enter on the Execution of his Office, he shall take the following Oath or Affirmation:--"I do solemnly swear (or affirm) that I will faithfully execute the Office of President of the United States, and will to the best of my Ability, preserve, protect and defend the Constitution of the United States."

Section 2.

The President shall be Commander in Chief of the Army and Navy of the United States, and of the Militia of the several States, when called into the actual Service of the United States; he may require the Opinion, in writing, of the principal Officer in each of the executive Departments, upon any Subject relating to the Duties of their respective Offices, and he shall have Power to grant Reprieves and Pardons for Offences against the United States, except in Cases of Impeachment.

He shall have Power, by and with the Advice and Consent of the Senate, to make Treaties, provided two thirds of the Senators present concur; and he shall nominate, and by and with the Advice and Consent of the Senate, shall appoint Ambassadors, other public Ministers and Consuls, Judges of the supreme Court, and all other Officers of the United States, whose Appointments are not herein otherwise provided for, and which shall be established by Law: but the Congress may by Law vest the Appointment of such inferior Officers, as they think proper, in the President alone, in the Courts of Law, or in the Heads of Departments.

The President shall have Power to fill up all Vacancies that may happen during the Recess of the Senate, by granting Commissions which shall expire at the End of their next Session.

Section 3.

He shall from time to time give to the Congress Information of the State of the Union, and recommend to their Consideration such Measures as he shall judge necessary and expedient; he may, on extraordinary Occasions, convene both Houses, or either of them, and in Case of Disagreement between them, with Respect to the Time of Adjournment, he may adjourn them to such Time as he shall think proper; he shall receive Ambassadors and other public Ministers; he shall take Care that the Laws be faithfully executed, and shall Commission all the Officers of the United States.

Section 4.

The President, Vice President and all civil Officers of the United States, shall be removed from Office on Impeachment for, and Conviction of, Treason, Bribery, or other high Crimes and Misdemeanors.

Article III

Section 1.

The judicial Power of the United States, shall be vested in one supreme Court, and in such inferior Courts as the Congress may from time to time ordain and establish. The Judges, both of the supreme and inferior Courts, shall hold their Offices during good Behaviour, and shall, at stated Times, receive for their Services, a Compensation, which shall not be diminished during their Continuance in Office.

Section 2.

The judicial Power shall extend to all Cases, in Law and Equity, arising under this Constitution, the Laws of the United States, and Treaties made, or which shall be made, under their Authority;--to all Cases affecting Ambassadors, other public Ministers and Consuls;--to all Cases of admiralty and maritime Jurisdiction;--to Controversies to which the United States shall be a Party;--to Controversies between two or more States;--between a State and Citizens of another State;--between Citizens of different States;--between Citizens of the same State claiming Lands under Grants of different States, and between a State, or the Citizens thereof, and foreign States, Citizens or Subjects.

In all Cases affecting Ambassadors, other public Ministers and Consuls, and those in which a State shall be Party, the supreme Court shall have original Jurisdiction. In all the other Cases before mentioned, the supreme Court shall have appellate Jurisdiction, both as to Law and Fact, with such Exceptions, and under such Regulations as the Congress shall make.

The Trial of all Crimes, except in Cases of Impeachment, shall be by Jury; and such Trial shall be held in the State where the said Crimes shall have been committed; but when not committed within any State, the Trial shall be at such Place or Places as the Congress may by Law have directed.

Section 3.

Treason against the United States, shall consist only in levying War against them, or in adhering to their Enemies, giving them Aid and Comfort. No Person shall be convicted of Treason unless on the Testimony of two Witnesses to the same overt Act, or on Confession in open Court.

The Congress shall have Power to declare the Punishment of Treason, but no Attainder of Treason shall work Corruption of Blood, or Forfeiture except during the Life of the Person attainted.

Article IV

Section 1.

Full Faith and Credit shall be given in each State to the public Acts, Records, and judicial Proceedings of every other State. And the Congress may by general Laws prescribe the Manner in which such Acts, Records, and Proceedings shall be proved, and the Effect thereof.

Section 2.

The Citizens of each State shall be entitled to all Privileges and Immunities of Citizens in the several States.

A Person charged in any State with Treason, Felony, or other Crime, who shall flee from Justice, and be found in another State, shall on Demand of the executive Authority of the State from which he fled, be delivered up, to be removed to the State having Jurisdiction of the Crime.

No Person held to Service or Labour in one State, under the Laws thereof, escaping into another, shall, in Consequence of any Law or Regulation therein, be discharged from such Service or Labour, but shall be delivered up on Claim of the Party to whom such Service or Labour may be due.

Section 3.

New States may be admitted by the Congress into this Union; but no new States shall be formed or erected within the Jurisdiction of any other State; nor any State be formed by the Junction of two or more States, or Parts of States, without the Consent of the Legislatures of the States concerned as well as of the Congress.

The Congress shall have Power to dispose of and make all needful Rules and Regulations respecting the Territory or other Property belonging to the United States; and nothing in this Constitution shall be so construed as to Prejudice any Claims of the United States, or of any particular State.

Section 4.

The United States shall guarantee to every State in this Union a Republican Form of Government, and shall protect each of them against Invasion; and on Application of the Legislature, or of the Executive (when the Legislature cannot be convened) against domestic Violence.

Article V

The Congress, whenever two thirds of both Houses shall deem it necessary, shall propose Amendments to this Constitution, or, on the Application of the Legislatures of two thirds of the several States, shall call a Convention for proposing Amendments, which, in either Case, shall be valid to all Intents and Purposes, as Part of this Constitution, when ratified by the Legislatures of three fourths of the several States, or by Conventions in three fourths thereof, as the one or the other Mode of Ratification may be proposed by the Congress; Provided that no Amendment which may be made prior to the Year One thousand eight hundred and eight shall in any Manner affect the first and fourth Clauses in the Ninth Section of the first Article; and that no State, without its Consent, shall be deprived of its equal Suffrage in the Senate.

Article VI

All Debts contracted and Engagements entered into, before the Adoption of this Constitution, shall be as valid against the United States under this Constitution, as under the Confederation.

This Constitution, and the Laws of the United States which shall be made in Pursuance thereof; and all Treaties made, or which shall be made, under the Authority of the United States, shall be the supreme Law of the Land; and the Judges in every State shall be bound thereby, any Thing in the Constitution or Laws of any State to the Contrary notwith-standing.

The Senators and Representatives before mentioned, and the Members of the several State Legislatures, and all executive and judicial Officers, both of the United States and of the several States, shall be bound by Oath or Affirmation, to support this Constitution; but no religious Test shall ever be required as a Qualification to any Office or public Trust under the United States.

Article VII

The Ratification of the Conventions of nine States, shall be sufficient for the Establishment of this Constitution between the States so ratifying the Same.

Done in Convention by the Unanimous Consent of the States present the Seventeenth Day of September in the Year of our Lord one thousand seven hundred and Eighty seven and of the Independence of the United States of America the Twelfth

In witness whereof We have hereunto subscribed our Names,

George Washington--President and deputy from Virginia

New Hampshire:
John Langdon, Nicholas Gilman

Massachusetts:
Nathaniel Gorham, Rufus King

Connecticut:
William Samuel Johnson, Roger Sherman

New York:
Alexander Hamilton

New Jersey:
William Livingston, David Brearly, William Paterson, Jonathan Dayton

Pennsylvania:
Benjamin Franklin, Thomas Mifflin, Robert Morris, George Clymer, Thomas FitzSimons, Jared Ingersoll, James Wilson, Gouverneur Morris

Delaware:
George Read, Gunning Bedford, Jr., John Dickinson, Richard Bassett, Jacob Broom

Maryland:
James McHenry, Daniel of Saint Thomas Jenifer, Daniel Carroll

Virginia:
John Blair, James Madison, Jr.

North Carolina
William Blount, Richard Dobbs Spaight, Hugh Williamson

South Carolina:
John Rutledge, Charles Cotesworth Pinckney, Charles Pinckney, Pierce Butler

Georgia:
William Few, Abraham Baldwin

Letter of Transmittal In Convention. Monday September 17th 1787.

Present The States of New Hampshire, Massachusetts, Connecticut, Mr. Hamilton from New York, New Jersey, Pennsylvania, Delaware, Maryland, Virginia, North Carolina, South Carolina and Georgia.

Resolved, That the preceeding Constitution be laid before the United States in Congress assembled, and that it is the Opinion of this Convention, that it should afterwards be submitted to a Convention of Delegates, chosen in each State by the People thereof, under the Recommendation of its Legislature, for their Assent and Ratification; and that each Convention assenting to, and ratifying the Same, should give Notice thereof to the United States in Congress assembled. Resolved, That it is the Opinion of this Convention, that as soon as the Conventions of nine States shall have ratified this Constitution, the United States in Congress assembled should fix a Day on which Electors should be appointed by the States which shall have ratified the same, and a Day on which the Electors should assemble to vote for the President, and the Time and Place for commencing Proceedings under this Constitution.

That after such Publication the Electors should be appointed, and the Senators and Representatives elected: That the Electors should meet on the Day fixed for the Election of the President, and should transmit their Votes certified, signed, sealed and directed, as the Constitution requires, to the Secretary of the United States in Congress assembled, that the Senators and Representatives should convene at the Time and Place assigned; that the Senators should appoint a President of the Senate, for the sole Purpose of receiving, opening and counting the Votes for President; and, that after he shall be chosen, the Congress, together with the President, should, without Delay, proceed to execute this Constitution.

Letter of Transmittal to the President of Congress

In Convention. Monday September 17th 1787. SIR:

We have now the honor to submit to the consideration of the United States in Congress assembled, that Constitution which has appeared to us the most advisable.

The friends of our country have long seen and desired that the power of making war, peace, and treaties, that of levying money, and regulating commerce, and the correspondent executive and judicial authorities, should be fully and effectually vested in the General Government of the Union; but the impropriety of delegating such extensive trust to one body of men is evident: hence results the necessity of a different organization.

It is obviously impracticable in the Federal Government of these States to secure all rights of independent sovereignty to each, and yet provide for the interest and safety of all. Individuals entering into society must give up a share of liberty to preserve the rest. The magnitude of the sacrifice must depend as well on situation and circumstance, as on the object to be obtained. It is at all times difficult to draw with precision the line between those rights which must be surrendered, and those which may be preserved; and, on the present occasion, this difficulty was increased by a difference among the several States as to their situation, extent, habits, and particular interests.

In all our deliberations on this subject, we kept steadily in our view that which appears to us the greatest interest of every true American, the consolidation of our Union, in which is involved our prosperity, felicity, safety--perhaps our national existence. This important consideration, seriously and deeply impressed on our minds, led each State in the Convention to be less rigid on points of inferior magnitude than might have been otherwise expected; and thus, the Constitution which we now present is the result of a spirit of amity, and of that mutual deference and concession, which the peculiarity of our political situation rendered indispensable.

That it will meet the full and entire approbation of every State is not, perhaps, to be expected; but each will, doubtless, consider, that had her interest alone been consulted, the consequences might have been particularly disagreeable or injurious to others; that it is liable to as few exceptions as could reasonably have been expected, we hope and believe; that it may promote the lasting welfare of that Country so dear to us all, and secure her freedom and happiness, is our most ardent wish.

With great respect, we have the honor to be, SIR, your excellency's most obedient and humble servants:

GEORGE WASHINGTON, President.

By the unanimous order of the convention. His Excellency the President of Congress.

Congress OF THE United States begun and held at the City of New-York, on Wednesday the fourth of March, one thousand seven hundred and eighty nine.

THE Conventions of a number of the States, having at the time of their adopting the Constitution, expressed a desire, in order to prevent misconstruction or abuse of its powers, that further declaratory and restrictive clauses should be added: And as extending the ground of public confidence in the Government, will best ensure the beneficent ends of its institution.

RESOLVED by the Senate and House of Representatives of the United States of America, in Congress assembled, two thirds of both Houses concurring, that the following Articles be proposed to the Legislatures of the several States, as amendments to the Constitution of the United States, all, or any of which Articles, when ratified by three fourths of the said Legislatures, to be valid to all intents and purposes, as part of the said Constitution; viz.

ARTICLES in addition to, and Amendment of the Constitution of the United States of America, proposed by Congress, and ratified by the Legislatures of the several States, pursuant to the fifth Article of the original Constitution.12

(Articles I through X are known as the Bill of Rights) ratified

Article the first.

After the first enumeration required by the first Article of the Constitution, there shall be one Representative for every thirty thousand, until the number shall amount to one hundred, after which, the proportion shall be so regulated by Congress, that there shall be not less than one hundred Representatives, nor less than one Representative for every forty thousand persons, until the number of Representatives shall amount to two hundred, after which the proportion shall be so regulated by Congress, that there shall not be less than two hundred Representatives, nor more than one Representative for every fifty thousand persons.

-

Article the second.

No law, varying the compensation for the services of the Senators and Representatives, shall take effect, until an election of Representatives shall have intervened. see Amendment XXVII

Article I

Congress shall make no law respecting an establishment of religion, or prohibiting the free exercise thereof; or abridging the freedom of speech, or of the press; or the right of the people peaceably to assemble, and to petition the Government for a redress of grievances.

Article II

A well regulated Militia, being necessary to the security of a free State, the right of the people to keep and bear Arms, shall not be infringed.

Article III

No Soldier shall, in time of peace be quartered in any house, without the consent of the Owner, nor in time of war, but in a manner to be prescribed by law.

Article [IV]

The right of the people to be secure in their persons, houses, papers, and effects, against unreasonable searches and seizures, shall not be violated, and no Warrants shall issue, but upon probable cause, supported by Oath or affirmation, and particularly describing the place to be searched, and the persons or things to be seized.

Article [V]

No person shall be held to answer for a capital, or otherwise infamous crime, unless on a presentment or indictment of a Grand Jury, except in cases arising in the land or naval forces, or in the Militia, when in actual service in time of War or public danger; nor shall any person be subject for the same offence to be twice put in jeopardy of life or limb; nor shall be compelled in any criminal case to be a witness against himself, nor be deprived of life, liberty, or property, without due process of law; nor shall private property be taken for public use, without just compensation.

Article [VI]

In all criminal prosecutions, the accused shall enjoy the right to a speedy and public trial, by an impartial jury of the State and district wherein the crime shall have been committed, which district shall have been previously ascertained by law, and to be informed of the nature and cause of the accusation; to be confronted with the witnesses against him; to have compulsory process for obtaining witnesses in his favor, and to have the Assistance of Counsel for his defence.

Article [VII]

In Suits at common law, where the value in controversy shall exceed twenty dollars, the right of trial by jury shall be preserved, and no fact tried by a jury, shall be otherwise re-examined in any Court of the United States, than according to the rules of the common law.

Article [VIII]

Excessive bail shall not be required, nor excessive fines imposed, nor cruel and unusual punishments inflicted.

Article [IX]

The enumeration in the Constitution, of certain rights, shall not be construed to deny or disparage others retained by the people.

Article [X]

The powers not delegated to the United States by the Constitution, nor prohibited by it to the States, are reserved to the States respectively, or to the people.

(end of the Bill of Rights)

[Article XI]

The Judicial power of the United States shall not be construed to extend to any suit in law or equity, commenced or prosecuted against one of the United States by Citizens of another State, or by Citizens or Subjects of any Foreign State.

[Article XII]

The Electors shall meet in their respective states, and vote by ballot for President and Vice-President, one of whom, at least, shall not be an inhabitant of the same state with themselves; they shall name in their ballots the person voted for as President, and in distinct ballots the person voted for as Vice-President, and they shall make distinct lists of all persons voted for as President, and of all persons voted for as Vice-President, and of the number of votes for each, which lists they shall sign and certify, and transmit sealed to the seat of the government of the United States, directed to the President of the Senate;--The President of the Senate shall, in the presence of the Senate and House of Representatives, open all the certificates and the votes shall then be counted;--The person having the greatest number of votes for President, shall be the President, if such number be a majority of the whole number of Electors appointed; and if no person have such majority, then from the persons having the highest numbers not exceeding three on the list of those voted for as President, the House of Representatives shall choose immediately, by ballot, the President. But in choosing the President, the votes shall be taken by states, the representation from each state having one vote; a quorum for this purpose shall consist of a member or members from two-thirds of the states, and a majority of all the states shall be necessary to a choice. And if the House of Representatives shall not choose a President whenever the right of choice shall devolve upon them, before the fourth day of March next following, then the Vice-President shall act as President, as in the case of the death or other constitutional disability of the President.14 --The person having the greatest number of votes as Vice-President, shall be the Vice-President, if such number be a majority of the whole number of Electors appointed, and if no person have a majority, then from the two highest numbers on the list, the Senate shall choose the Vice-President; a quorum for the purpose shall consist of two-thirds of the whole number of Senators, and a majority of the whole number shall be necessary to a choice. But no person constitutionally ineligible to the office of President shall be eligible to that of Vice-President of the United States.

Article XIII

Neither slavery nor involuntary servitude, except as a punishment for crime whereof the party shall have been duly convicted, shall exist within the United States, or any place subject to their jurisdiction. Congress shall have power to enforce this article by appropriate legislation.

Article XIV

1. All persons born or naturalized in the United States, and subject to the jurisdiction thereof, are citizens of the United States and of the State wherein they reside. No State shall make or enforce any law which shall abridge the privileges or immunities of citizens of the United States; nor shall any State deprive any person of life, liberty, or property, without due process of law; nor deny to any person within its jurisdiction the equal protection of the laws.
2. Representatives shall be apportioned among the several States according to their respective numbers, counting the whole number of persons in each State, excluding Indians not taxed. But when the right to vote at any election for the choice of electors for President and Vice President of the United States, Representatives in Congress, the Executive and Judicial officers of a State, or the members of the Legislature thereof, is denied to any of the male inhabitants of such State, being twenty-one years of age,15 and citizens of the United States, or in any way abridged, except for participation in rebellion, or other crime,

the basis of representation therein shall be reduced in the proportion which the number of such male citizens shall bear to the whole number of male citizens twenty-one years of age in such State.

3. No person shall be a Senator or Representative in Congress, or elector of President and Vice President, or hold any office, civil or military, under the United States, or under any State, who, having previously taken an oath, as a member of Congress, or as an officer of the United States, or as a member of any State legislature, or as an executive or judicial officer of any State, to support the Constitution of the United States, shall have engaged in insurrection or rebellion against the same, or given aid or comfort to the enemies thereof. But Congress may by a vote of two-thirds of each House, remove such disability.
4. The validity of the public debt of the United States, authorized by law, including debts incurred for payment of pensions and bounties for services in suppressing insurrection or rebellion, shall not be questioned. But neither the United States nor any State shall assume or pay any debt or obligation incurred in aid of insurrection or rebellion against the United States, or any claim for the loss or emancipation of any slave; but all such debts, obligations and claims shall be held illegal and void.
5. The Congress shall have power to enforce, by appropriate legislation, the provisions of this article.

Article XV

The right of citizens of the United States to vote shall not be denied or abridged by the United States or by any State on account of race, color, or previous condition of servitude.

The Congress shall have power to enforce this article by appropriate legislation.

Article XVI

The Congress shall have power to lay and collect taxes on incomes, from whatever source derived, without apportionment among the several States, and without regard to any census or enumeration.

[Article XVII]

1. The Senate of the United States shall be composed of two Senators from each State, elected by the people thereof, for six years; and each Senator shall have one vote. The electors in each State shall have the qualifications requisite for electors of the most numerous branch of the State legislatures. affects 3
2. When vacancies happen in the representation of any State in the Senate, the executive authority of such State shall issue writs of election to fill such vacancies: Provided, That the legislature of any State may empower the executive thereof to make temporary appointments until the people fill the vacancies by election as the legislature may direct.
3. This amendment shall not be so construed as to affect the election or term of any Senator chosen before it becomes valid as part of the Constitution.

Article [XVIII]16

1. After one year from the ratification of this article the manufacture, sale, or transportation of intoxicating liquors within, the importation thereof into, or the exportation thereof from the United States and all territory subject to the jurisdiction thereof for beverage purposes is hereby prohibited.
2. The Congress and the several States shall have concurrent power to enforce this article by appropriate legislation.
3. This article shall be inoperative unless it shall have been ratified as an amendment to the Constitution by the legislatures of the several States, as provided in the Constitution, within seven years from the date of the submission hereof to the States by the Congress.

Article [XIX]

The right of citizens of the United States to vote shall not be denied or abridged by the United States or by any State on account of sex.

Congress shall have power to enforce this article by appropriate legislation.

Article [XX]

1. The terms of the President and Vice President shall end at noon on the 20th day of January, and the terms of Senators and Representatives at noon on the 3d day of January, of the years in which such terms would have ended if this article had not been ratified; and the terms of their successors shall then begin.
2. The Congress shall assemble at least once in every year, and such meeting shall begin at noon on the 3d day of January, unless they shall by law appoint a different day.
3. If, at the time fixed for the beginning of the term of the President, the President elect shall have died, the Vice President elect shall become President. If a President shall not have been chosen before the time fixed for the beginning of his term, or if the President elect shall have failed to qualify, then the Vice President elect shall act as President until a President shall have qualified; and the Congress may by law provide for the case wherein neither a President elect nor a Vice President elect shall have qualified, declaring who shall then act as President, or the manner in which one who is to act shall be selected, and such person shall act accordingly until a President or Vice President shall have qualified.
4. The Congress may by law provide for the case of the death of any of the persons from whom the House of Representatives may choose a President whenever the right of choice shall have devolved upon them, and for the case of the death of any of the persons from whom the Senate may choose a Vice President whenever the right of choice shall have devolved upon them.
5. Sections 1 and 2 shall take effect on the 15th day of October following the ratification of this article.
6. This article shall be inoperative unless it shall have been ratified as an amendment to the Constitution by the legislatures of three-fourths of the several States within seven years from the date of its submission.

Article [XXI]

1. The eighteenth article of amendment to the Constitution of the United States is hereby repealed.
2. The transportation or importation into any State, Territory, or possession of the United States for delivery or use therein of intoxicating liquors, in violation of the laws thereof, is hereby prohibited.
3. This article shall be inoperative unless it shall have been ratified as an amendment to the Constitution by conventions in the several States, as provided in the Constitution, within seven years from the date of the submission hereof to the States by the Congress.

Amendment XXII

1. No person shall be elected to the office of the President more than twice, and no person who has held the office of President, or acted as President, for more than two years of a term to which some other person was elected President shall be elected to the office of the President more than once. But this article shall not apply to any person holding the office of President when this article was proposed by the Congress, and shall not prevent any person who may be holding the office of President, or acting as President, during the term within which this article becomes operative from holding the office of President or acting as President during the remainder of such term.
2. This article shall be inoperative unless it shall have been ratified as an amendment to the Constitution by the legislatures of three-fourths of the several states within seven years from the date of its submission to the states by the Congress.

Amendment XXIII

1. The District constituting the seat of government of the United States shall appoint in such manner as the Congress may direct: A number of electors of President and Vice President equal to the whole number of Senators and Representatives in Congress to which the District would be entitled if it were a state, but in no event more than the least populous state; they shall be in addition to those appointed by the states, but they shall be considered, for the purposes of the election of President and Vice President, to be electors appointed by a state; and they shall meet in the District and perform such duties as provided by the twelfth article of amendment.

2. The Congress shall have power to enforce this article by appropriate legislation.

Amendment XXIV

1. The right of citizens of the United States to vote in any primary or other election for President or Vice President, for electors for President or Vice President, or for Senator or Representative in Congress, shall not be denied or abridged by the United States or any state by reason of failure to pay any poll tax or other tax.
2. The Congress shall have power to enforce this article by appropriate legislation.

Amendment XXV

1. In case of the removal of the President from office or of his death or resignation, the Vice President shall become President.
2. Whenever there is a vacancy in the office of the Vice President, the President shall nominate a Vice President who shall take office upon confirmation by a majority vote of both Houses of Congress.
3. Whenever the President transmits to the President pro tempore of the Senate and the Speaker of the House of Representatives his written declaration that he is unable to discharge the powers and duties of his office, and until he transmits to them a written declaration to the contrary, such powers and duties shall be discharged by the Vice President as Acting President.
4. Whenever the Vice President and a majority of either the principal officers of the executive departments or of such other body as Congress may by law provide, transmit to the President pro tempore of the Senate and the Speaker of the House of Representatives their written declaration that the President is unable to discharge the powers and duties of his office, the Vice President shall immediately assume the powers and duties of the office as Acting President.

Thereafter, when the President transmits to the President pro tempore of the Senate and the Speaker of the House of Representatives his written declaration that no inability exists, he shall resume the powers and duties of his office unless the Vice President and a majority of either the principal officers of the executive department or of such other body as Congress may by law provide, transmit within four days to the President pro tempore of the Senate and the Speaker of the House of Representatives their written declaration that the President is unable to discharge the powers and duties of his office. Thereupon Congress shall decide the issue, assembling within forty-eight hours for that purpose if not in session. If the Congress, within twenty-one days after receipt of the latter written declaration, or, if Congress is not in session, within twenty-one days after Congress is required to assemble, determines by two-thirds vote of both Houses that the President is unable to discharge the powers and duties of his office, the Vice President shall continue to discharge the same as Acting President; otherwise, the President shall resume the powers and duties of his office.

Amendment XXVI

1. The right of citizens of the United States, who are 18 years of age or older, to vote, shall not be denied or abridged by the United States or any state on account of age.
2. The Congress shall have the power to enforce this article by appropriate legislation.

Amendment XXVII

No law varying the compensation for the services of the Senators and Representatives shall take effect until an election of Representatives shall have intervened.

Appendix C

Naturalization Exam for Citizenship Test and Questions

Learn About the United States – Quick Civic Lessons for the Naturalization Test U.S. Citizen and Immigration Services

1. What is the supreme law of the land?
2. What does the Constitution do?
3. The idea of self-government is in the first three words of the Constitution. What are these words?
4. What is an amendment?
5. What do we call the first ten amendments to the Constitution?
6. What is one right or freedom from the First Amendment?
7. How many amendments does the Constitution have?
8. What did the Declaration of Independence do?
9. What are two rights in the Declaration of Independence?
10. What is freedom of religion?
11. What is the economic system in the United States?
12. What is the "rule of law"?
13. Name one Branch or part of government.
14. What stops one branch of government from becoming too powerful?
15. Who is in charge of the executive branch?
16. Who makes federal laws?
17. What are the two parts of the U.S. Congress
18. How many U.S. Senators are there?
19. We elect a U.S. Senator for how many years?
20. What is one of your state's U.S. Senators now?
21. The House of Representatives has how many voting members?
22. We elect a U.S. Representative for how many years?
23. Name your U.S. Representative.
24. Who does a U.S. Senator represent?
25. Why do some states have more Representatives than other states?
26. We elect a President for how many years?
27. In what month do we vote for President?
28. What is the name of the President of the United States now?
29. What is the name of the Vice President of the United States now?
30. If the President can no longer serve, who becomes President?
31. If both of the President and the Vice President can no longer serve, who becomes President?

32. Who is the Commander in Chief of the military?
33. Who Signs bills to become laws?
34. Who vetoes bills?
35. What does the President's Cabinet do?
36. What are two Cabinet-level positions?
37. What does the judicial branch do?
38. What is the highest court in the United States?
39. How many justices are on the Supreme Court?
40. Who is the Chief Justice of the United States?
41. Under our Constitution, some powers belong to the federal government. What is one power of the federal government?
42. Under our Constitution, some powers belong to the states. What is one power of the states?
43. Who is the Governor of your state now?
44. What is the capital of your state?
45. What are the two major political parties in the United States?
46. What is the political party of the President now?
47. What is the name of the Speaker of the House of Representatives now?
48. There are four amendments to the Constitution about who can vote. Describe one of them.
49. What is one responsibility that is only for United States citizens?
50. Name one right only for United States citizens.
51. What are two rights of everyone living in the United States?
52. What do we show loyalty to when we say the Pledge of Allegiance?
53. What is one promise you make when you become a United States citizen?
54. How old do citizens have to be to vote for President?
55. What are two ways that Americans can participate in their democracy?
56. When is the last day you can send in federal income tax forms?
57. When must all men register for the Selective service?
58. What is one reason colonists came to America?
59. Who lived in America before the Europeans arrived?
60. What group of people was taken to America and sold as slaves?
61. Why did colonists fight the British?
62. Who wrote the Declaration of Independence?
63. When was the Declaration of Independence adopted?
64. There were 13 original states. Name three.
65. What happened at the Constitutional Convention?
66. When was the Constitution written?
67. The Federalist Papers supported the passage of the U.S. Constitution. Name one of the writers.
68. What is one thing Benjamin Franklin is famous for?
69. Who is the "Father of Our Country"?
70. Who was the first President?
71. What territory did the United States buy from France in 1803?

72. Name one war fought by the United States in the 1800s.
73. Name the U.S. war between the North and the South.
74. Name one problem that led to the Civil War.
75. What was one important thing that Abraham Lincoln did?
76. What did the Emancipation Proclamation do?
77. What did Susan B. Anthony do?
78. Name one war fought by the United States in the 1900s.
79. Who was President during World War I?
80. Who was President during the Great Depression and World War II?
81. Who did the United States fight in World War II?
82. Before he was President, Eisenhower was a general. What war was he in?
83. During the Cold War, what was the main concern of the United States?
84. What movement tried to end racial discrimination?
85. What did Martin Luther King, Jr. do?
86. What major event happened on September 11, 2001, in the United States?
87. Name one American Indian tribe in the United States.
88. Name one of the two longest rivers in the United States.
89. What ocean is on the West Coast of the United States?
90. What ocean is on the East Coast of the United States?
91. Name one U.S. territory.
92. Name one state that borders Canada.
93. Name one state that borders Mexico.
94. What is the capital of the United States?
95. Where is the Statue of Liberty?
96. Why does the flag have 13 stripes?
97. Why does the flag have 50 stars?
98. What is the name of the national anthem?
99. When do we celebrate Independence Day?
100. Name two national U.S. holidays.

Appendix D

Patriotic Songs

Star Spangled Banner & Songs

Oh, say can you see by the dawn's early light
What so proudly we hailed at the twilight's last gleaming?
Whose broad stripes and bright stars thru the perilous fight,
O'er the ramparts we watched were so gallantly streaming?
And the rocket's red glare, the bombs bursting in air,
Gave proof through the night that our flag was still there.
Oh, say does that star-spangled banner yet wave
O'er the land of the free and the home of the brave?

On the shore, dimly seen through the mists of the deep,
Where the foe's haughty host in dread silence reposes,
What is that which the breeze, o'er the towering steep,
As it fitfully blows, half conceals, half discloses?
Now it catches the gleam of the morning's first beam,
In full glory reflected now shines in the stream:
'Tis the star-spangled banner! Oh long may it wave
O'er the land of the free and the home of the brave!

And where is that band who so vauntingly swore
That the havoc of war and the battle's confusion,
A home and a country should leave us no more!
Their blood has washed out their foul footsteps' pollution.
No refuge could save the hireling and slave
From the terror of flight, or the gloom of the grave:
And the star-spangled banner in triumph doth wave
O'er the land of the free and the home of the brave

Oh! thus be it ever, when freemen shall stand
Between their loved home and the war's desolation!
Blest with victory and peace, may the heav'n rescued land
Praise the Power that hath made and preserved us a nation.
Then conquer we must, when our cause it is just,
And this be our motto: "In God is our trust."
And the star-spangled banner in triumph shall wave
O'er the land of the free and the home of the brave!

America the Beautiful

O beautiful for spacious skies, For amber waves of grain,
For purple mountain majesties Above the fruited plain!
America! America! God shed his grace on thee
And crown thy good with brotherhood From sea to shining sea!

O beautiful for pilgrim feet Whose stern impassioned stress
A thoroughfare of freedom beat Across the wilderness!
America! America! God mend thine every flaw,
Confirm thy soul in self-control, Thy liberty in law!

O beautiful for heroes proved In liberating strife.
Who more than self their country loved And mercy more than life!
America! America! May God thy gold refine
Till all success be nobleness And every gain divine!

O beautiful for patriot dream That sees beyond the years
Thine alabaster cities gleam Undimmed by human tears!
America! America! God shed his grace on thee
And crown thy good with brotherhood From sea to shining sea!

O beautiful for halcyon skies, For amber waves of grain,
For purple mountain majesties Above the enameled plain!
America! America! God shed his grace on thee
Till souls wax fair as earth and air And music-hearted sea!

O beautiful for pilgrims feet, Whose stem impassioned stress
A thoroughfare for freedom beat Across the wilderness!
America! America! God shed his grace on thee
Till paths be wrought through wilds of thought By pilgrim foot and knee!

O beautiful for glory-tale Of liberating strife
When once and twice, for man's avail
Men lavished precious life! America! America!
God shed his grace on thee Till selfish gain no longer stain
The banner of the free!

O beautiful for patriot dream That sees beyond the years
Thine alabaster cities gleam Undimmed by human tears!
America! America! God shed his grace on thee
Till nobler men keep once again Thy whiter jubilee!

My Country, 'Tis of Thee

My country tis of thee, Sweet land of liberty
Of thee I sing.
Land where my fathers died! Land of the Pilgrim's pride!
From every mountainside Let Freedom Ring

My native country, thee, Land of the noble free,
Thy name I love.
I love the rocks and rills, Thy woods and templed hills;
My heart with rapture fills Like that above.

Let music swell the breeze, And ring from all the trees
Sweet freedom's song.
Let mortal tongues awake; Let all that breathe partake;
Let rocks their silence break, The song prolong.
Our father's God to, Thee, Author of liberty,
To Thee we sing.
Long may our land be bright With freedom's holy light;
Protect us by Thy might, Great God, our King!

The Battle Hymn of the Republic

Mine eyes have seen the glory of the coming of the Lord;
He is trampling out the vintage where the grapes of wrath are stored;
He hath loosed the fateful lightning of His terrible swift sword:
His truth is marching on.

(Chorus)
Glory, glory, hallelujah!
Glory, glory, hallelujah!
Glory, glory, hallelujah!
His truth is marching on.

I have seen Him in the watch-fires of a hundred circling camps,
They have builded Him an altar in the evening dews and damps;
I can read His righteous sentence by the dim and flaring lamps:
His day is marching on.

(Chorus)

I have read a fiery gospel writ in burnished rows of steel:
"As ye deal with my condemners, so with you my grace shall deal";
Let the Hero, born of woman, crush the serpent with his heel,
Since God is marching on.

(Chorus)

He has sounded forth the trumpet that shall never call retreat;
He is sifting out the hearts of men before His judgment-seat:
Oh, be swift, my soul, to answer Him! be jubilant, my feet!
Our God is marching on.

(Chorus)

In the beauty of the lilies Christ was born across the sea,
With a glory in His bosom that transfigures you and me.
As He died to make men holy, let us die to make men free,
While God is marching on.

(Chorus)

He is coming like the glory of the morning on the wave,
He is Wisdom to the mighty, He is Succour to the brave,
So the world shall be His footstool, and the soul of Time His slave,
Our God is marching on.

(Chorus)

Appendix E

On the Patriot's Path

"Never doubt that a small group of thoughtful, committed citizens can change the world. Indeed, it is the only thing that ever has."
- Margaret Mead

Making the Pledge

As patriots, we must pledge our hearts, minds, strength, honor, fortune, and even our lives to God, to the constitution, to the cause of liberty and to one another. God promises us prosperity and happiness if we strive to keep this pledge. If we deviate from the path this pledge keeps us on, we have no promise.

A Few Degrees

On a beautiful day in 1979, when 257 passengers boarded their jet plane in New Zealand anticipating an exciting round trip sightseeing flight of Antarctica, no one, including the pilots, was aware that someone had made a mistake in the flight coordinates. The error was only two degrees, but it ended up causing the plane to be 28 miles (45 kilometers) to the east of their assumed destination. The pilots were experienced, but had no way of knowing that the incorrect coordinates had placed them directly in the path of a 12,000 foot (3,700 meters) tall active volcano called Mount Erebus.

As the plane crossed over the coastline of Antarctica, the pilots descended to give the passengers a better view of the landscape. Everyone on board, including the pilots, was impressed with the beautiful white of the snow and ice below. The white landscape blended in with the white of the clouds above. It looked like they were flying over flat ground.

When the instruments began to sound the warning, the pilots began checking their instruments and coordinates. However, the ground was rapidly rising, and when they realized what was happening, it was too late. The plane crashed into the mountain, and everyone was killed. This terrible tragedy was caused by someone making a mistake of only two degrees. In his documentary *Mount Erebus Plane Crash*, Arthur Marcel teaches us some valuable lessons.

Small Errors Greatly Impact the Course of History

Many great civilizations of the past have been destroyed because the masses chose to follow leaders who were off by only two degrees. In the beginning, it is very difficult to discern any problems, even though we are not on the right course. The longer the journey, the more off course we get. The road to prosperity, power, progress, and political ideology are vital. However, if their aim is off target by just two degrees, they can result in tragedy and tyranny.

Eliminating just two words "in God" will change our whole focus and direction. Adding just two amendments (beginning with 2% tax, two senators) has put America on a dangerous course and has disrupted the balance of power. Just two Supreme Court decisions legalizing abortion and pornography have altered the course of our moral society.

During my life, I have learned that the difference between our liberty or our bondage, freedom or socialism, a government by, for, and of the people or a dictatorial or tyrannical government results from errors of only a few degrees. No one wants to experience conflict, civil unrest, or even war.

What Lessons Can We Learn?

Small errors and minor drifts away from the constitution will always result in consolidation of power. Minor decisions can lead to major consequences. It is critically important to keep all constitutional checks and balances in place. The government will not correct these errors unless they are forced to do so. The citizens must insist on disciplined government and make the corrections themselves. The longer corrective action is delayed, the greater the problems become, and the more difficult the changes are to make. Disaster is always on the horizon.

We must be courageous and correct the problems. We must be vigilant and cautious and heed the early warning signals, and then be a warning voice to others. We must avoid debt. We must be well prepared and protected. We must be patriots, self-reliant and defenders of liberty. If we become spectators and leave our destiny in the hands of others, who may knowingly or unknowingly make small but fatal errors, then we get what we deserve.

Campaign Slogans

From whom do we get our country back? What course are we supposed to get back on? What is causing the spiraling problems we face? Who is robbing us of our freedom?

These are all questions I ask when I hear politicians and citizens of all parties make promising statements, but offer no definitive answers. I'm convinced that we, as individuals and as a nation, have the answers and the solutions. The United States of America has a purpose and destiny and a map to guide us. What we need are individuals who follow the map and are immovable in their determination to stay the course. Our map is the U.S. Constitution, and our purpose and destiny is to remain a good and a free people.

All the other rhetoric about prosperity and progress mean very little if we are moving in the wrong direction. Being powerful, wealthy, and being the biggest and the best are only hollow campaign slogans if we are on a course to self-destruction. Putting these slogans into practice may just accelerate us in the wrong direction.

Getting Off Course

Our country got off course when individuals and organizations began to use the federal government for unconstitutional purposes. Attempts were made from the very beginning, but more so just before and after the Civil War. (Read NOW speech #14, *Not Yours to Give*). During the decades before and after, the world saw a dramatic increase in popularity of socialism, ideology, and activism. Much of it took root in the fabric of our nation.

The country was connected from sea to sea by railroad and telegraph. Opportunities were unlimited, and there seemed to be a carefree optimism at the beginning of the twentieth century as government expanded and morality declined.

In 1913, the 16th amendment was adopted giving the federal government "taxation without limitation." That same year the 17th amendment took away the state's balance of power.

These two amendments crippled our nation by consolidating power. The federal government no longer had to get revenues from the states, and senators no longer had to answer to their state legislatures. This dramatically moved us away from the intended republic formed by our Founding Fathers towards a pure democracy, which was never intended.

In 1920, following World War I, the League of Nations was organized to prevent war through collective security and disarmament and to resolve international disputes through negotiation and arbitration. This socialistic approach to a one-world government failed miserably, but was revived after World War II when the United Nations was organized on April 120, 1946.

Meanwhile, the socialist agenda was being pushed forward with the Social Security Act of 1935. The original intent was to collect 2% on the first $3,000 earned for a retirement safety net. In 1937 $1,278,000 was paid out to 53,236 beneficiaries. By 2008, there were 50,898,244 beneficiaries, with $615,344,000 paid. In 2013, the federal government collected 12.4% on the first $113,700. We now find ourselves in a socialist country trying to keep up with other socialist countries.

The first Food Stamp Program was enacted into law on May 16, 1939. It was supposed to help the unfortunate during the Great Depression, but it has evolved into permanent debilitating programs promoting apathy and dependency. Many other welfare programs have been created that touch and influence every citizen and industry.

The reader has to spend but a few hours reading about the origin of the many federal agencies and departments that have been established since 1913. Almost every president since then, and most citizens, have accepted these programs and departments as an important part of our federal government. Each election, candidates and voters argue about issues to solve our nation's problems. Few understand or speak out about getting to the real root of these problems.

So, how do we get our country back on course? How do we solve serious problems and remain free? First, we must read the map and correct the errors that have been made. We must get out of debt and then stay the course. This means that we must first understand and follow the U.S. Constitution. We must measure every politician's ideas and actions by this constitutional standard and elect only those who are disciplined and resist the temptation to accumulate or exercise more power or influence. We must evaluate every piece of legislation by this same standard. We must immediately repeal the 16th and 17th amendments along with any others that give more power to the federal government. We cannot do anything to undermine the sovereignty of the United States or the inalienable rights of our citizens.

We Must Correct Our Course

We are not doomed to a tragic end. We can change the course of history. Our founding fathers did this, and we can do it, too. We must have a plan and quickly correct the mistakes made long ago. In summary, we must immediately implement the "Patriot's Path: The Plan & Solution," including the following:

1. Elect those who will uphold and defend the U.S. Constitution as the supreme law of the land.
2. Repeal the 16th Amendment and end taxation without limitation.
3. Repeal the 17th Amendment and give the states back their voice and balance of power in government.

4. Dramatically reduce spending and eliminate the national debt.
5. Restructure the federal government to do only what the constitution empowers them to do.
6. Strengthen military weapons and troops; care for veterans.
7. Promote increased legal immigration and eliminate illegal immigration.
8. Establish a Composite Commodity Standard and audit or replace the Federal Reserve.
9. Become energy and manufacturing independent.
10. Phase out all federal social and welfare programs to be administered by the states.

This is how we get back on the "Patriot's Path." This is how we save and uphold the constitution. This is how we take our nation back and solve the problems we face. We can do it. We must do it. We are the United States of America.

* * *

Now that you have read this *Appendix E* and Speech #14 *Not Yours to Give – Davey Crockett*, I enthusiastically invite you to read the whole book from start to finish.

Join with me to make a point and win the presidency.

www.ingramcontent.com/pod-product-compliance
Lightning Source LLC
Chambersburg PA
CBHW060839280326
41934CB00007B/840